SELF-SUFFICIENCY

SELF-SUFFICIENCY

A guide for 21st-century living

Alan & Gill Bridgewater

Contents

Foreword

'I went to the woods because I wished to live deliberately, to confront only the essential facts of life, and see if I could not learn what it had to teach, and not, when I came to die, discover that I had not lived.' So said Henry David Thoreau, explaining why he decided to move to Walden Pond and live in a hut.

When Gill and I look at the world … the air thick with pollution, our forests shrinking, carbon emissions rising, global warming a measurable fact, people working under stress so that they can purchase meaningless consumerables – we see that chaos rules. Our way of tackling the problem is not to try to change the world, or even to try to change our immediate community, but rather to change the way that we – Gill and I – live in the world. Being self-sufficient is central to this change.

Thousands of people are happy to spend a lifetime arguing the pros and cons of the state of the world and self-sufficiency. They say things like it does not work, it is selfish, it is head in the sand, it is no more than scratching around trying to make ends meet, it is elitism, and so on. Gill and I have neither the time nor the inclination to argue about whether the world is in a mess or who is responsible for the mess, nor indeed do we want to debate the size, shape and colour of the mess. We just want to 'turn on, tune in and drop out' and experience the unique therapeutic pleasures of working our patch.

Our aim in this book is to demonstrate that the simplest answer to what we see as 'consumerism gone rogue' is for all of us to live life on a smaller, more personal, practical human scale. For us, self-sufficiency equates with self-reliance, which in turn equates with independence and self-fulfilment. We have no illusions that it is possible to make our living from the land or be completely self-sufficient, nor do we want to just sit back and play the blame game. Trying to be more self-sufficient – working with our hands building sheds, shelters and structures, generating some part of our energy, growing crops, cutting wood, storing produce, cooking home-grown food, recycling, doing craft work and managing our geese and bees – not only soothes us and gives us a feeling of strength, confidence and well-being, but we also find it liberating, exciting, challenging and good old-fashioned fun. If you are fed up with the endless talking about how you could lead a greener, more rewarding life, and want to get down to the joyous hands-on business of actually living such a life, just keep reading.

Alan Bridgewater

Living the dream

When I was a kid in the late 1950s, I dreamed about being a rugged, explorer-type hero. In my granny's various sheds and outhouses in the country, I was Daniel Defoe's Robinson Crusoe living on his desert island; in the woods and swampy meadows around my home, I was Rider Haggard's African adventurer Allan Quatermain; and so on. For me, every shed, shack and shelter was a stockade on a desert island, and every patch of scrubby wilderness was a forest to be explored.

It was much the same for Gill, who spent a lot of her childhood living in a corrugated tin shack in the country. She also enjoyed being self-reliant and self-contained. It was not surprising, I suppose, that when Gill and I met at art school in the early 1960s we swiftly got together and picked up on the talk about self-sufficiency. Very soon after leaving college, we put an advert in the press that ran: 'Isolated cottage wanted – must be set in its own ground'.

One moment we were living in a nice cottage complete with all the trimmings (including our first baby) and the next we were living in a redbrick ruin of a farmhouse, in the middle of a field, with no running water, no electricity – in fact nothing much apart from space, silence and a feeling of peace. It seems funny, looking back, that when we first arrived at Valley Farm House we were happily able to live in our isolated shell of a house – no carpets on the floor or plaster on the walls and our nights lit by candles and firelight – without any worries about money or possessions. As for our plans at that time, it was all so easy (we were still in our twenties) – we would rebuild the house, set the barn up as a pottery and weaving workshop, sort out the water supply, and generally establish our own little self-sufficient paradise.

So, in what seems like a lifetime later, where are we now? The kids have grown up and are heading in another direction, and Gill and I are having a joyous and challenging time working our patch. As for the world, it is far more complex and many times more polluted and impoverished than we ever imagined. It has not been easy, and our long and winding road has revealed all sorts of physical and emotional pitfalls, but Gill and I are now living our dream. It is not quite nirvana, not quite 'the highest happiness', and we have had to make many compromises, but it works for us.

We have a small, wooden shack-like house set in 1.6 hectares (4 acres) of field and woodland, and we are still doing our best to be self-sufficient – not much in and not much out. Having been teachers, potters and weavers, and having kept sheep, goats, chickens, turkeys and donkeys, we now have a flock of geese, three hives of bees, a beautiful orchard, a very fruitful raised bed and a no-dig vegetable garden, and we earn money writing about our various garden, craft and eco adventures. The walls and attics of our little wooden home are stuffed with hemp insulation, there is a passive glass conservatory along the sunny side, a wood-fired stove chugs away through the winter, there is a huge solar water heater on the roof, we are just about to fit a bank of photovoltaic panels to provide some part of our electricity, we have an old tractor that serves us well, and we are encircled by a group of like-minded friends.

All that said, if ever there was a time to try for self-sufficiency, then this is it. Not only is the subject of self-sufficiency prominent in people's thinking, but all the technologies that would make off-grid self-reliance more readily achievable are all around us. Power from the sun, wind, water, earth and sea — just about everything is possible. We understand that nirvana is as much in the head as anywhere, and no doubt things will, for us at least, get much more difficult as we get older, but for Gill and me the journey is much more meaningful than the destination. It may sound a bit trite, but this is how we see it.

So what next? We will increase the number of hives, we will continue selling eggs and honey at the gate, and swapping our produce and knowhow for logs, manure, tractor repairs and such like, we will explore the possibilities of geothermal heating, and we will continue working towards what we have come to think of as a relaxed self-reliance. Be mindful, when you read this book, that it is not some sort of long-headed dissertation on gardening or cookery or farming, nor do we see it as being an evangelistic eco treatise or tirade, but rather it is simply a coming-together of our story and our experiences and ambitions, that we hope will show you how it is possible in a relaxed, fun, hard-working way to produce some of your own food and energy. So you might never achieve, or even want to achieve, complete self-sufficiency, but our hope is that you will be more contented and more independent in the trying.

As for all those critics who are forever scratching, blogging, texting and tweeting about what they see as the impossibilities of self-sufficiency, just leave them be, or, as my grandpa would have said, 'Don't worry — their own wind will blow them away!'

Land

Dream property

Dream property Although we knew from the start that we wanted to live in the country and be self-sufficient, we also knew that the only way forward for us was to become teachers and then to use the teaching position as a stepping-stone. The teaching job was easy enough: one moment we were at college and living in a London flat and the next we were deep in the country living in a mansion teaching 'troubled' girls. The difficulty was that we had no real idea as to the 'shape' of our dream home, other than it had to be isolated.

After a great deal of searching, we settled on a cottage at the edge of a village. While we very soon discovered that the village location was wrong, it gave us a benchmark from which to work. On the strength of fast-rising property prices, we put our house up for sale and started a search for our 'isolated cottage'. A week later, we were standing in front of our dream – a redbrick ruin of a house with a low cow-house to the side of the house, lots of tumbledown lean-tos and outhouses, acres of knee-deep thistles and mountains of mud and manure. The floors were covered in manure, there were holes in the roof, everything was dark and smelling of damp and decay – it was perfect! The first night was one of those once-in-a-lifetime moments, with us in bed in the tumbledown barn, the baby and dogs nicely settled, the second baby just about to happen and nothing much else but a night-black silence.

How to proceed

Your move will be life-changing. Run your vision through your mind until you have a clear understanding of your needs. Do not worry about details, just focus on the big picture. Draw up a questionnaire (see left): If you are unsure about committing yourself, spend at least six months in the chosen area to see how it pans out. Run the trial through the winter.

Make sure that all rights of way are to your advantage. You need to know if you or your neighbours have rights of way for water pipes and cables. Can you pipe water from the nearest river or supply, and can a neighbouring farmer run any pipes or cables under or over your land? Ownership of all boundaries, fences, bridges and gates must be set out on your legal deeds. You need to know who is responsible for the upkeep of all the fences, hedges, walls, ditches and gates. Make sure that the widths of gates are clearly described and defined.

A good water supply is vital. An off-grid property is autonomous – it does not rely on utilities. If you are thinking about buying an off-grid property, you need to know how, from day one, you are going to cope with cooking, heating and drinking. Start by solving the problem of drinking water, and take it from there.

QUESTIONNAIRE

1   Do you want to settle in your mother country?
2   Do you need meadows for cows, space for a kiln, or anything else?
3   What sort of land are you after: woodland, riverside, seashore?
4   Are all parties in agreement?
5   Are you happy to rebuild, live in a mobile home, build a shack, camp out, or adopt some other living arrangements?
6   Are you going to continue working?
7   How are you going to fund your adventure?

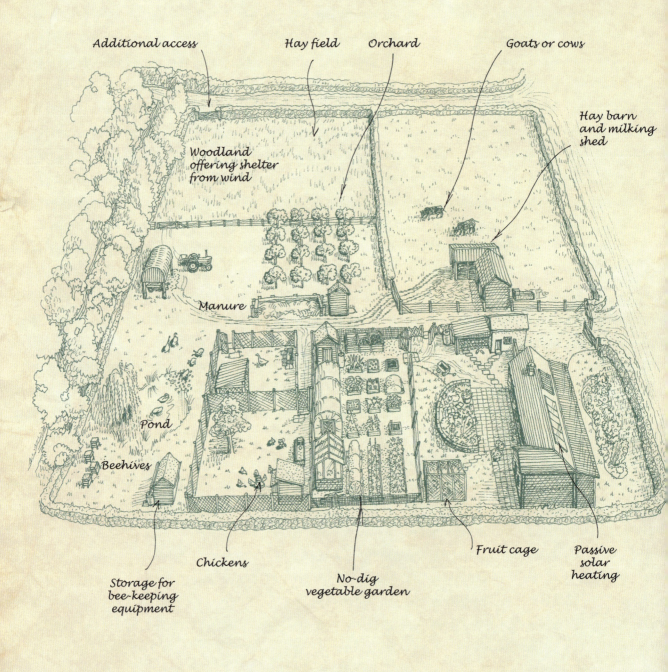

IDEAL SMALLHOLDING OR HOMESTEAD

Additional access

Hay field

Orchard

Goats or cows

Hay barn
and milking
shed

Woodland
offering shelter
from wind

Manure

Pond

Beehives

Storage for
bee-keeping
equipment

Chickens

No-dig
vegetable garden

Fruit cage

Passive
solar
heating

Town self-sufficiency

The scenario is that you are living in town, and wondering whether you can in some way be self-sufficient without moving to the country.

Concrete self-sufficiency

We know a young couple who moved from London to a mobile-home-type property on the outskirts where the enclosed garden was covered by concrete and corrugated-iron chicken sheds. Undaunted, they recycled the iron sheds to make raised beds, set them on the concrete slabs, and filled them up with the chicken manure. Now they have a vegetable garden, chickens and bees, and they have planning permission to build a small single-storey eco home. Everyone is happy, including the local council and the neighbours.

Railway tunnel self-sufficiency

We have friends who live in an end-of-terrace house that backs onto a disused railway goods yard. They lease the house, goods yard, a stretch of railway line, and the derelict tunnel from the railway company. They have chickens, a large vegetable plot, a small mushroom farm in the tunnel, lots of rabbits, several colonies of bees, and two goats.

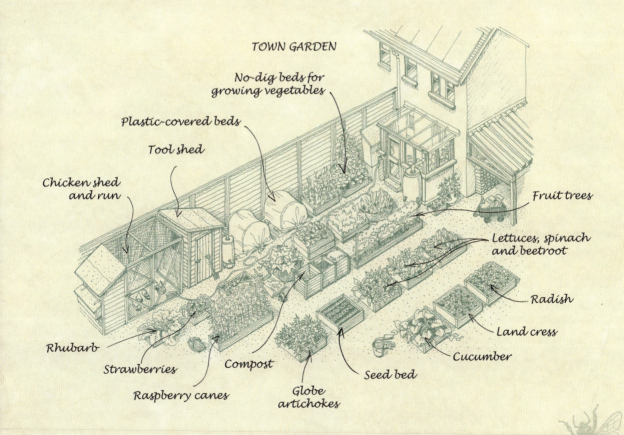

TOWN GARDEN

No-dig beds for growing vegetables

Plastic-covered beds

Tool shed

Chicken shed and run

Fruit trees

Lettuces, spinach and beetroot

Radish

Land cress

Cucumber

Rhubarb

Strawberries

Raspberry canes

Compost

Globe artichokes

Seed bed

A place in the country

The problem with many self-sufficiency 'wannabes' is that they are bombarded by the media with reality programmes and articles that feature eco-green, good-life living so that they have a skewed, rose-tinted vision of what is possible. If you are a 'townie' and are thinking about self-sufficiency in the country, look beyond those cute pictures of kids stroking sheep and forever-laughing girls slow-motioning through meadows – they are all smoke and mirrors.

QUESTIONS TO ASK YOURSELF

1   Are you going to enjoy the full drama of the changing seasons – snow, rain, drought, wind?

2   If you have kids, will you be happy to drive them to school, or to the nearest town to see their friends?

3   Are you going to miss the hum and buzz of the town?

4   Are you going to enjoy living in a small community where you might become the focus of attention?

5   Will you be happy to give animals around-the-clock attention?

6   Will you be content to swap dry pavements for mud, streetlights for darkness, the cinema for the village hall, and your city-slicker trainers for wellies?

A place in a foreign country

Although Gill and I know for sure that living in England is our only option, there was a time when we seriously considered moving to rural France. In many ways it would have been logical – the property was cheaper, we could do our bookwork over the internet, and the climate is easy. After lots of self-questioning, we came to the conclusion that as we knew very little about the French language, law, customs and traditions it was actually a very bad idea.

We knew three couples at that time who had moved abroad: one to Italy to run a craft school, one to Spain to join a commune, and one to Greece. The message that came back to us over the years was that it is not a good idea to go to another country thinking that you can move to a farm, or other property, and do your own thing in isolation. You have to learn the language and fully adopt your new country. You must see your shift as a life-long commitment.

MORE FOR YOUR MONEY ABROAD?

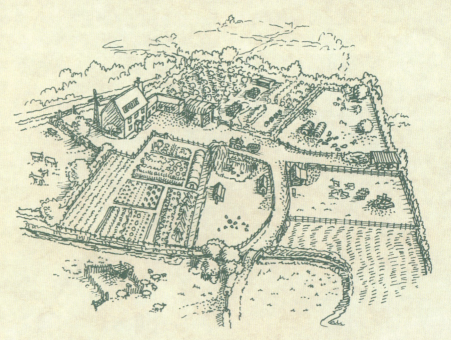

House

Eco self-sufficient Gaia house

This is a house that is environmentally friendly in terms of technologies and materials. It sits easily in the environment, is efficient in its use of energy, does not push out waste, is self-sustaining, is safe and clean, is not too hot, cold, dry or humid, and is constructed of non-toxic, local materials.

Our house

When Gill and I bought our current house, we were presented with a modest, single-storey, shed-like wooden structure that was built in about the 1920s. After thinking through various options, we decided that the best first step with our limited budget was to repair the basic structure and to maximize the insulation as we went along. Over the first year we fitted a new roof, removed and replaced the old exterior timber cladding, stuffed the cavities with foil-faced foam insulation, and fitted new double-glazed windows. We then worked on the interior walls, stuffing the cavities with hemp insulation and facing the inside walls with a breathable membrane topped with tongue-and-groove board. We then built a passive solar room, along the sunny side of the house, that pushed hot air in and out of the house, and finally we fitted a solar water system and a log-burning stove. We are now fitting a batch of photovoltaic panels to supply lighting and power. Later we plan to fit a composting toilet and a rainwater-harvesting system. Since most people will opt for upgrading rather than moving, the following work plan will point the way.

Work plan and questions to ask yourself

- INSULATION Could you increase the insulation by cladding and insulate the walls on the outside? Or could you insulate both inside and outside?

- WINDOWS Most old windows let heat out and cold winds in – could you upgrade your windows or fit heavy curtains and/or shutters?

- DOORS Most exterior doors leak precious heat – could you reduce the number of exterior doors? Could you fit a porch to create a sort of air lock?

- FLOORS If you have solid concrete floors and high ceilings, could you add a layer of rigid foam insulation topped with a wooden floor on top of existing floors? If you have a suspended wooden floor, you could either top it as described, or you could lift the boards and fit insulation between the joists.

- ROOF Could you fit foil-faced foam insulation between the roof joists and/or stuff the attic with insulation?

THE GAIA HOUSE

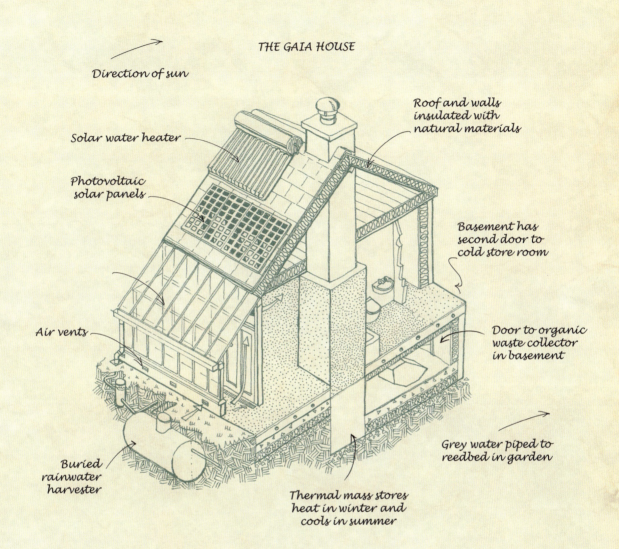

Direction of sun

Solar water heater

Photovoltaic
solar panels

Roof and walls
insulated with
natural materials

Basement has
second door to
cold store room

Air vents

Door to organic
waste collector
in basement

Buried
rainwater
harvester

Thermal mass stores
heat in winter and
cools in summer

Grey water piped to
reedbed in garden

- PASSIVE SOLAR HEATING Could you add a long, low conservatory along the sun-facing side of the house?

- SOLAR PANELS FOR HOT WATER Could you add a solar water heater?

- PHOTOVOLTAIC PANELS Could you cut costs by fitting such a system to provide electricity?

Passive solar house
This is a house that uses passive solar energy systems to maintain a comfortable indoor climate. The two primary elements are its direct-gain design and its indirect-gain Trombe wall. The wonderful thing about a passive solar house of this design and character is its silent simplicity – the sun shines and the house heats and cools itself, all without complex electro-mechanical whizz-bangs.

Direct-gain solar design
Whoever said 'let the sunshine in' must surely have been thinking about direct solar gain. The system is elegantly simple and direct. Big glass windows set in the walls of the house are located so that they face the sun at midday. The sun rises and shines, and the walls, floors and structures (the storage mass within the house) absorb and store the heat. The sun sinks and sets, and the storage mass slowly gives out heat to maintain a comfortable temperature.

Indirect-gain Trombe wall
In essence, a Trombe wall is a massive sun-facing wall that is separated from the outdoors by glazing and an air space. Trombe walls absorb solar energy and release it selectively to either warm or ventilate the interior space within the house. The sun shines through the glazing to heat the masonry walls – the Trombe storage mass – so that the space between the glazing and the wall becomes a thermal chimney. Flap-covered vents set at floor and ceiling level in both the glass wall and the Trombe walls are arranged so that currents of hot air that rise by convection between the wall and glass can be directed either in or out of the building. Two key points are: (1) the structure needs to face the sun at midday; and (2) the walls and floors must be made of heat-absorbing materials such as brick and stone.

Our passive solar house
Having decided that we liked the simple elegance of passive solar heating, the problem for us was how to build such a system into our existing wooden house. After much thought, we built a long, greenhouse-type structure along the sun-facing side. Within our 'glass place', we built Trombe-inspired brick walls, a large raised brick bed that we filled to the brim with waste copper pipe topped with shingle, and an insulated concrete floor topped with bricks. There are vents along the bottom of the glass place, and windows and vents that run from the glass place through into the house.

When the sun shines, the brick structures within the glass place absorb the heat; when the sun sets, the heat is slowly given out. Depending upon our needs, we can: open the windows to let heat into the house; close windows and open vents to release heat from the glass place into the great outdoors; or open vents in the glass place and windows in both sides of the house to create a cooling air flow. Certainly, it is all a bit 'Heath Robinson' – lots of flaps and vents – but it works.

A PASSIVE SOLAR HOUSE IN WINTER

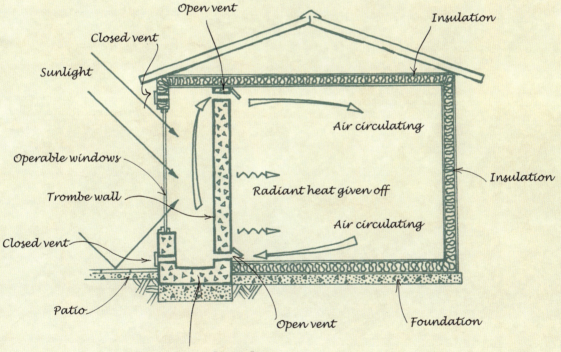

'Earth, wind and sun' house

Since the Industrial Revolution, communities have been forced to reject tried-and-trusted traditions and techniques. Thatch and stone have been ousted by corrugated iron and concrete, and brick and wood have been replaced by plaster and plastic. Even the dimensions and scale now relate more to mechanized manufacturing than to the builder's needs.

The way it was and could be

A natural 'earth, wind and sun' house is a house where everything is in harmony with the environment. The natural house is by definition modest, and as far as possible built from local materials. Such a house harks back to a time when house builders had no other choice than to use time-honoured building technologies and materials.

Traditionally, the builder would choose his site, make sure that there was a source of clean water, check that the site was sheltered from prevailing winds and set to face the sun at midday (or in some regions with the windows facing away from the sun), maybe ensure that there was space for his sons to build, and then start work. The wood came from the local forest, the clay and stone came from nearby pits and quarries, the thatch came from local reedbeds or wheatfields, and so on.

As different districts were low-lying, mountainous, and rich in stone, clay, flint, slate, reeds, oak, softwood or some other material, so the character, form and structure of the houses mirrored the areas in which they were built. The houses reflected the climate, topography, geology, farming practices, and so on; they perfectly fitted the environment because they were *of* the environment.

The new natural house takes a fresh look at traditional tools and at local materials and technologies. The key words here are modest, local, passive, healthy and harmonious.

Hippy recycled house

When we were art students in the mid-1960s, the American hippy movement was just beginning. With its roots in the 1950s beatnik movement, the earlier bohemians, and the even earlier German folk Wandervogel ('migratory birds') movement in the 1900s, the main push of the hippies was their counterculture lifestyle. They questioned everything: politics, transport, religion, what we ate, how we dressed, sex codes, marriage, and of course housing. Although it was in the interests of industry and the establishment to crush the hippy movement, the good news is that it is alive and thriving.

Make-do-and-mend hippy houses

The exciting thing about the hippy approach to housing is the way that they have taken the natural 'back-to-the-land' philosophy that encourages the use of natural materials and given it an eco-recycling twist that advocates also using waste products like car tyres, bottles, aluminium drinks cans, cardboard, oil drums, plastic sheets, bits of cars and all the other stuff that would otherwise be dumped into landfill. Strangely, while my grandpa had to make-do-and-mend because he was poor and because manufactured materials were difficult to come by, Gill and I are now doing much the same thing because we live in a rich society that is awash with waste manufactured materials.

Our twist on hippy housing

In much the same way as Robinson Crusoe started by stripping his wrecked ship of rope, iron, fabrics, copper cable and such like, and then built his house using a mix of salvaged materials and whatever natural materials he could find on the island, we have reworked and refurbished our traditional rural home using a mix of natural found materials and recycled industrial materials. We have used old bricks for the floors, salvaged doors and timbers for some of the interiors, salvaged metal and plastic containers in the vegetable garden, and used bits of this and that for some of the fences and gates. We have salvaged timber and metal sheeting to make garden sheds and shelters, used offcuts and giveaways from timber yards for some of the decorative details, and used old wheels to make garden carts and bits salvaged from ships for lighting and windows. You may be thinking 'how restricting', but not so – it is an exciting challenge, it relieves the pressure on the environment, and it is a sound, money-saving philosophy.

Your way forward

Because recycling is gradually becoming mainstream, with architects and designers positively falling over themselves to use recycled materials, or 'low-carbon improvisational materials', your freedom to choose and use recycled materials will depend upon where you live. There is no problem in the Netherlands, some parts of the USA, in various off-grid rural communities around the world, and in some prestigious, forward-looking, eco-green developments in the UK, which are more than happy to see recycled materials being used. The difficulty comes in backward-looking communities that have aggressive and restrictive planning codes. The best advice is to research your area and then either protest or adjust your approach.

RECYCLED HOUSE

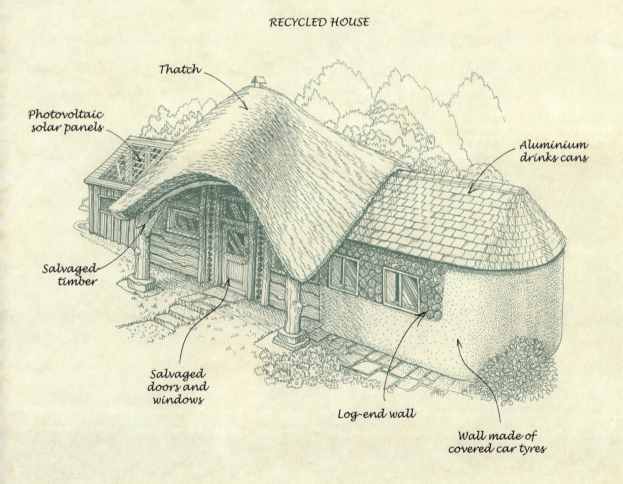

Thatch

Photovoltaic solar panels

Aluminium drinks cans

Salvaged timber

Salvaged doors and windows

Log-end wall

Wall made of covered car tyres

Energy

The way it is

Research suggests that when most people are questioned about the energy crisis – pollution, soaring energy costs, transporting oil and gas around the globe, the need to use renewable energy, possible cuts in supplies – they just say something feeble such as they are thinking about using low-energy light bulbs. In this climate of denial and lack of interest, the first step towards solving the problem is not somehow to get the deniers to acknowledge that such a problem does at least exist, but rather for you personally to take charge of your own energy needs. This is the perfect time for you to improve your own energy arrangements (such as fit a micro energy system or go off-grid).

If you still have doubts and are looking for an authoritive lead, it is on record that Queen Elizabeth II, Richard Branson, Bill Gates, Paul McCartney, the Rolling Stones, Johnny Depp and other prime movers are all going down their own off-grid road. They cannot be doing it to save money!

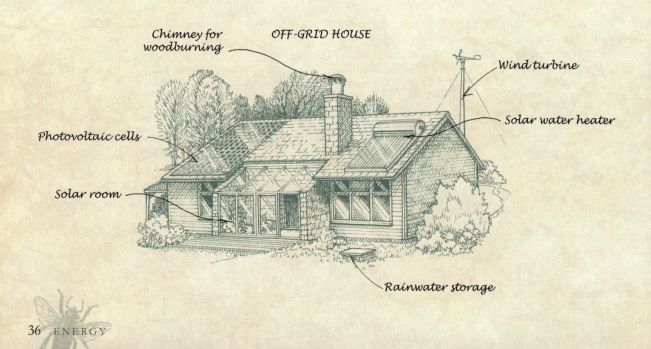

OFF-GRID HOUSE

Chimney for woodburning

Wind turbine

Solar water heater

Photovoltaic cells

Solar room

Rainwater storage

Reducing consumption

When Gill and I moved to this property, we had a small, regular income, lots of knowhow, plenty of time on our hands, and a clear determination to produce some of our own energy. We started by looking at what we had on the ground (the existing bottled heating, cooking, lighting) and then, in the light of our studies (what we had, what we needed and the order of work), we slowly made changes. In between writing and gardening, we repaired the basic structure of the house, fitted new windows, stuffed the cavities with insulation, replaced the gas with a woodburning stove, put a solar water heater on the roof, and fitted photovoltaic electrics. We are now reassessing what we have and are fine-tuning accordingly.

Thinking it through

Take a long look at your set-up (who you are, where you live, how you live, how you want to live, how much money you have, and so on) and run through the possibilities in your mind. When you have a clear understanding of your needs, draw up a mission plan – a list or a set of diagrams that outlines your intent.

REDUCING ENERGY USAGE

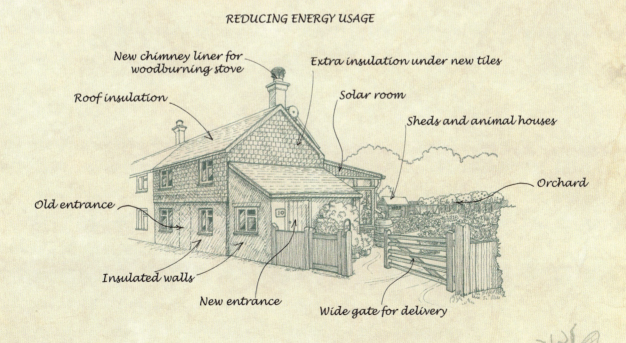

New chimney liner for woodburning stove

Extra insulation under new tiles

Roof insulation

Solar room

Sheds and animal houses

Orchard

Old entrance

Insulated walls

New entrance

Wide gate for delivery

Renewable energy

When I was a kid in the 1950s, we would visit my Welsh grandma. She cooked locally grown food on a wood-fired range, we sat around the range to keep warm, and when it was dark we lit lamps and candles. We were warm, dry, well fed and self-reliant.

The way it is

Now most people switch on electric lights, cook on stoves powered by electricity, gas and oil, and heat their homes by electricity, gas and oil – all non-renewable fossil fuels that are fast running out.

Small is beautiful

Although governments and industry are trying to work out how they can retain the status quo by investing in monolithic renewables (wind turbines, photovoltaic power stations, ocean wave-energy, hydro energy), up-and-running German and Swedish schemes show that if everyone installed small, stand-alone, renewable, natural-energy systems (solar-powered hot water heating, solar-powered generators, geothermal-powered air conditioners, wood-fired stoves for heating, rainwater catchment), then individual self-reliance would be for the greater self-sufficient good. We would have to make compromises and no doubt there would be environmental costs, but 'small is beautiful' is a viable, rational way of thinking.

RENEWABLE ENERGY OPTIONS

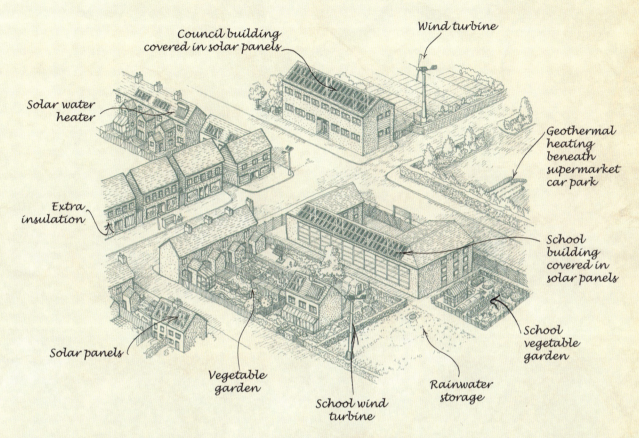

Council building covered in solar panels

Wind turbine

Solar water heater

Geothermal heating beneath supermarket car park

Extra insulation

School building covered in solar panels

Solar panels

Vegetable garden

School vegetable garden

School wind turbine

Rainwater storage

Woodburning

For us, a woodburning stove epitomizes self-sufficiency. In our mind's eye, we see a sequence of pictures and word associations: stove, logs, cabin, wilderness, forest, self-reliance, strength, cooking, stews, cosiness, warmth. We run our stove continuously from early winter to early spring. A typical morning in winter goes like this: get up, riddle the stove (sieve out the coals), put in more wood, have breakfast around the stove, put a baked potato or soup on the stove to cook, do work, have lunch around the stove. At night, I riddle the stove, fill it up with wood and turn down the air intake.

The options

- STANDARD STOVE used for heating living space

- STOVE WITH BACK BOILER used for heating living space and water

- COOKER used for heating living space, water and cooking

- FURNACE used for central heating

Good woods for burning

There are good and bad woods. The following list will give you some idea of what is possible.

- BEECH Middling choice; easy to saw and split, little smoke, good amount of heat, good to medium burn.

- BIRCH Good choice when dry; easy to saw and split, little smoke, lots of heat.

- CEDAR Good choice when dry; easy to saw and split, little smoke, beautiful smell, very noisy, fair amount of heat.

- OAK Very good choice; easy to saw and split, little or no smoke, lots of heat, long slow burn.

- WILLOW Poor choice; easy to saw and split, smoky, short burn, little heat.

Hints and tips

· Have a dry-powder fire extinguisher within reach.
· The chimney must be sound and regularly swept.
· If you keep the fire in overnight, start the day with a fierce burn to burn off dangerous tars.
· An uncharacteristic smoky burn indicates a blocked chimney – let the fire out and check it.

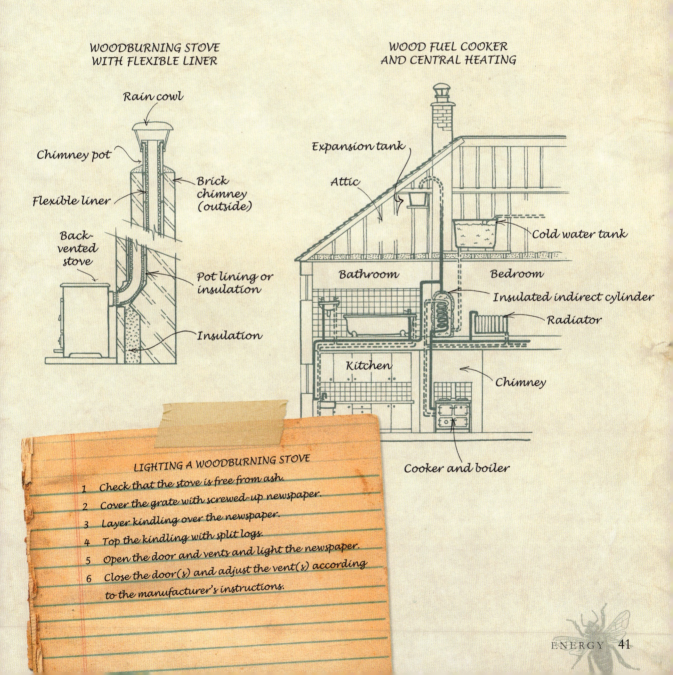

WOODBURNING STOVE
WITH FLEXIBLE LINER

Rain cowl

Chimney pot

Flexible liner

Back-vented stove

Brick chimney (outside)

Pot lining or insulation

Insulation

WOOD FUEL COOKER
AND CENTRAL HEATING

Expansion tank

Attic

Bathroom

Bedroom

Cold water tank

Insulated indirect cylinder

Radiator

Kitchen

Chimney

Cooker and boiler

LIGHTING A WOODBURNING STOVE

1 Check that the stove is free from ash.
2 Cover the grate with screwed-up newspaper.
3 Layer kindling over the newspaper.
4 Top the kindling with split logs.
5 Open the door and vents and light the newspaper.
6 Close the door(s) and adjust the vent(s) according to the manufacturer's instructions.

Lighting

In 1910 it was reckoned that a good lighting standard was 30 lux, in 1920 the standard was raised to 200 lux, and from the 1940s the lux levels kept on rising to a point where many homes now burn about 1500+ lux. Where we once strained our eyes in the gloom, we now strain our eyes because there is too much artificial light. If we go by current good health codes that recommend 300 lux, it follows that most people could quarter their costs simply by not switching on so many lights.

How Gill and I do it

Although we now have mains lighting, we have reduced consumption by changing all our bulbs to LEDs that have been evaluated as being the most energy-efficient lighting source so far. This saves up to 90% energy compared to traditional bulbs, and 50% compared to normal energy-saving bulbs. As for lifestyle changes, in summer we get up at dawn and go to bed at sundown, and in winter, when we are sitting around the log fire or television, we either do not bother with lights or we use a candle or lamp.

Photovoltaics

We have just fitted six photovoltaic panels that are wired through to an inverter, regulator and bank of batteries. We have set them up as a stand-alone off-grid system. We will start by using them for lighting, computers and so on, and then, if they prove their worth, we will double the number of panels in order to power larger pieces of equipment.

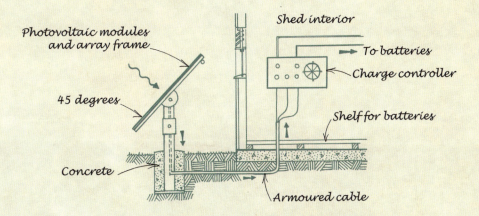

FREESTANDING PHOTOVOLTAIC SYSTEM

Photovoltaic modules and array frame

Shed interior

To batteries

Charge controller

45 degrees

Shelf for batteries

Concrete

Armoured cable

Water

At the beginning of the 20th century, most people carried water in buckets from a well to the house, or if they were lucky they had a hand-operated pump in the scullery. Because it was a horrible chore, they were mean with water. When people had a well, they used one or two buckets of water each per day; now in developed countries we use a staggering 30–100 buckets per person per day.

Rainwater

If you plan to live off-grid, you need a good supply of clean water. It is perfect if you have a well, spring, or clean river, but failing that the only other option is to store rainwater. The illustration shows a typical, traditional, brick and concrete rainwater filtering and storing system. There are many small, modern, easy-to-fit kit systems on the market.

Grey water

Grey water is all the water from the bath, shower and kitchen, meaning water that has been used but is free from faeces and food matter. Such water can be used to flush toilets.

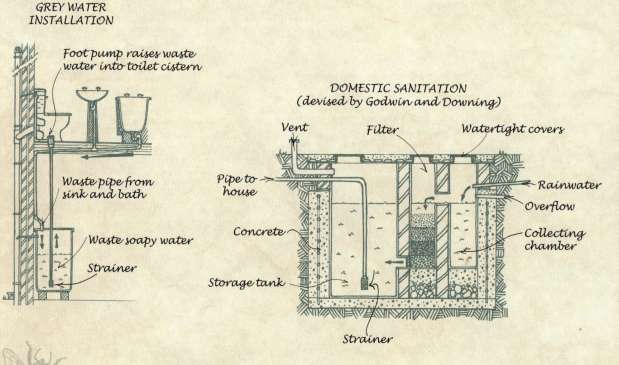

GREY WATER INSTALLATION

Foot pump raises waste water into toilet cistern

Waste pipe from sink and bath

Waste soapy water

Strainer

DOMESTIC SANITATION
(devised by Godwin and Downing)

Vent

Filter

Watertight covers

Pipe to house

Rainwater

Overflow

Concrete

Collecting chamber

Storage tank

Strainer

Toilet systems

When I was a kid in the 1950s, and later when we were at Valley Farm House in the 1970s, our toilet system was a basic affair that involved going into a brick outhouse or 'privy', sitting on a wooden shelf over a pit and then sieving earth over the offering. The privy was emptied into one of several pits at the far end of the garden and a year or so later the resulting compost was used on the vegetable patch.

Off-grid toilet options

• PRIVY If you are living well off the beaten track, a privy is a good option. Make sure that your chosen site complies with local codes, and that it is well away from your water supply.

• SEPTIC TANK Although a septic tank is a sound, traditional, easy-to-build system (really no more than an underground tank with a delivery pipe in and a soakaway pipe out) the downside is that it does not add to the greater good of your self-sufficient way of life.

• COMPOSTING TOILET This is a modern, room-sized system that can be fitted under the house or as a separate item in the garden. The kitchen and toilet waste goes into a closed container where, after a year or so, it breaks down into a friable, sweet-smelling garden compost.

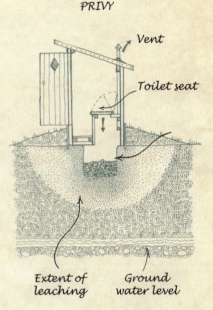

PRIVY

Vent

Toilet seat

Extent of leaching

Ground water level

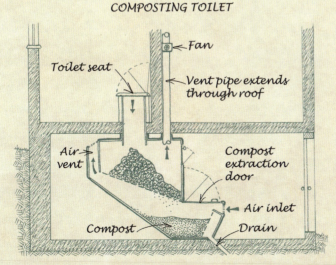

COMPOSTING TOILET

Fan

Toilet seat

Vent pipe extends through roof

Air vent

Compost extraction door

Air inlet

Compost

Drain

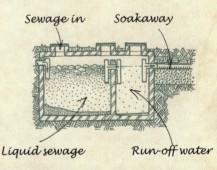

SEPTIC TANK

Sewage in

Soakaway

Liquid sewage

Run-off water

Solar energy

Solar energy In the context of this book, solar energy is the conversion of sunlight into: (1) space heating by means of direct solar gain; (2) water heating by means of solar collectors; and (3) electricity generation by means of photovoltaics (PVs). We all know about the basics: the sun rises and sets, it is warmer in summer than in winter, it is hottest at the middle of the day. It feels good to sit in the sun, as it warms our bodies and gives us an emotional and spiritual lift.

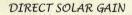

DIRECT SOLAR GAIN

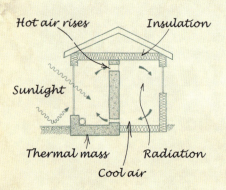

Hot air rises Insulation

Sunlight

Thermal mass Radiation

Cool air

Passive direct solar gain

In temperate climates, where temperature changes are relatively moderate, houses have long been designed to take advantage of direct solar gain. The sun shines in through sun-facing windows, where it is passively stored as heat energy, and windows, curtains, blinds and shutters are opened and closed to let hot air out or cool air in. A passive direct solar home takes best advantage of the direction of the sun, the shape of the landscape, trees, water, natural movements of heat and air – anything that will maintain a comfortable temperature. It is passive because it does not involve the use of electro-mechanical devices.

Indirect solar gain

Although this system uses much the same design principles and materials as direct solar gain, it ups the advantages by increasing the amount of thermal mass between the sun and the space being heated, and by positioning vents and ducts to control convection.

INDIRECT SOLAR GAIN

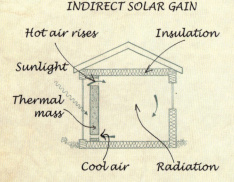

Hot air rises Insulation

Sunlight

Thermal mass

Cool air Radiation

Trombe walls

A Trombe wall system, named after French engineer Felix Trombe, takes the indirect solar gain system one step further by having a sun-facing wall separated from the outdoors by glazing and an air space, with vents at the top and bottom of the wall that run through into the living space. The sun shines through the glazing and onto the wall, and the space heats up and becomes a thermal chimney; at this point, vents and windows are opened and closed to increase airflow and to heat or cool the living space. The joy of this is its simplicity.

Solar hot water collectors

A solar hot water collector is a hot water system that is powered by direct solar energy. Although there are many systems on the market – flat collectors, wide-angle collectors and so on – we favour the Microsolar. We have two Microsolar units on our roof; if the sun shines, we get as much hot water as we need.

Solar photovoltaic panels

A typical photovoltaic (PV) off-grid system is made up of an array of panels, a battery charge controller, a bank of deep-cycle batteries, one or more inverters, and a range of cables, switches and cutouts. Sunlight goes in at one end and AC electricity comes out of the other.

MICROSOLAR COLLECTOR THERMOSYPHON
SOLAR WATER HEATER INSTALLATION

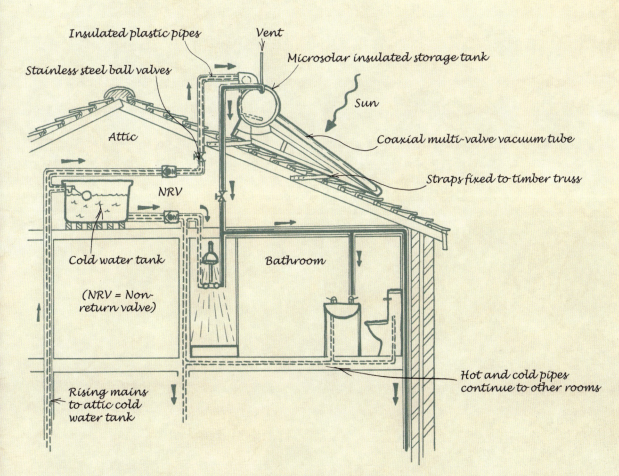

Insulated plastic pipes

Vent

Microsolar insulated storage tank

Stainless steel ball valves

Sun

Attic

Coaxial multi-valve vacuum tube

Straps fixed to timber truss

NRV

Cold water tank

Bathroom

(NRV = Non-return valve)

Hot and cold pipes continue to other rooms

Rising mains to attic cold water tank

Wind energy

Wind energy Although we have always seen small, stand-alone wind turbines as being a good option, personal experience tells us they are fraught with difficulties. The problem is not technical, because there are now many wonderfully efficient wind turbines, but they seem to polarize communities into those who love them and those who see them as a threat. If you live in an isolated windy area well away from trees and anxious neighbours, then a wind turbine is a logical option.

Insulation

Insulation If you are planning to be self-sufficient, and as you proceed cut costs and generally be more self-reliant, insulating your home is the perfect launching point. I am not talking about a feeble extra centimetre or so of insulation in the attic; I am talking about making war on energy waste and stuffing insulation, foam, fibre glass, bubble-foil, wool, hemp or whatever you choose into every crevice and cranny – in the attic, under the floor, in the walls, layer upon layer of insulation, as much as you can push in, until the house stops leaking energy.

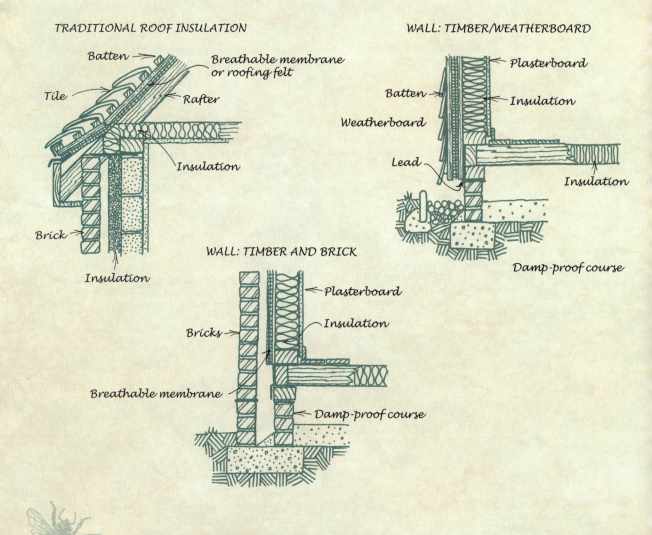

TRADITIONAL ROOF INSULATION

Batten
Breathable membrane or roofing felt
Tile
Rafter
Insulation
Brick
Insulation

WALL: TIMBER/WEATHERBOARD

Plasterboard
Batten
Insulation
Weatherboard
Lead
Insulation
Damp-proof course

WALL: TIMBER AND BRICK

Plasterboard
Insulation
Bricks
Breathable membrane
Damp-proof course

Recycling Not so long ago, most of our household throw-outs were reused. Paper, metal and fabrics were recycled within the household or collected as salvage, wood ash and coal cinders were used in the garden, and just about everything else was composted or reworked in and around the house. Now we are all gradually burying ourselves under mountains of rubbish – plastic containers, metal drinks cans, glass bottles, plastic toys, clothes, furniture, batteries, computers, food and kitchen waste. Most people's waste bins are overflowing. We cannot turn the clocks back, nor can we worry about people and industries who seem hell-bent on gliding to glory on vast rafts of rubbish; the best we as individuals can do is tidy up our own lives.

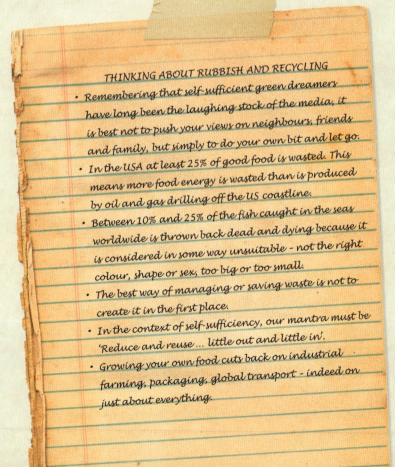

THINKING ABOUT RUBBISH AND RECYCLING

- Remembering that self-sufficient green dreamers have long been the laughing stock of the media, it is best not to push your views on neighbours, friends and family, but simply to do your own bit and let go.
- In the USA at least 25% of good food is wasted. This means more food energy is wasted than is produced by oil and gas drilling off the US coastline.
- Between 10% and 25% of the fish caught in the seas worldwide is thrown back dead and dying because it is considered in some way unsuitable - not the right colour, shape or sex, too big or too small.
- The best way of managing or saving waste is not to create it in the first place.
- In the context of self-sufficiency, our mantra must be 'Reduce and reuse ... little out and little in'.
- Growing your own food cuts back on industrial farming, packaging, global transport - indeed on just about everything.

Growing food

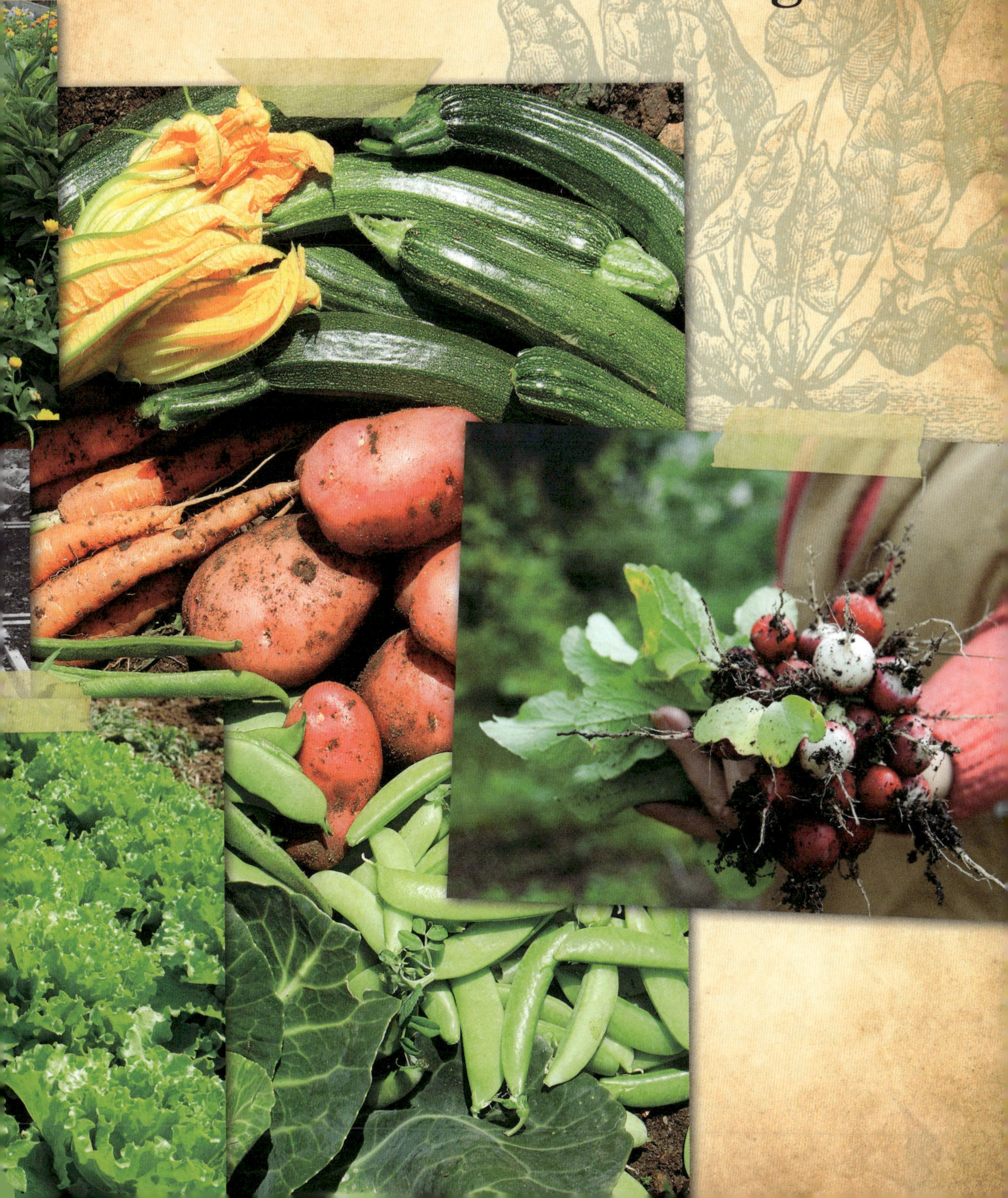

Growing food the no-dig way

Whatever the size, shape and character of your self-sufficiency set-up, if you want to grow your own food, an organic raised bed no-dig garden is perfect. The initial set-up will involve you in a lot of work (building timber beds, bringing in farmyard manure and spent mushroom compost, fencing), but once you have the basic no-dig structures in place it will be relatively easy. Imagine no more digging, spending a lifetime trying to improve the underlying soil, or using chemical cure-alls – just you, the no-dig system, self-sufficiency and plenty of good clean produce.

Moreover, if you are prepared to go one step further and keep livestock, such as chickens, sheep or cows, and compost all your own kitchen waste, you will be able to achieve a self-contained, eco-friendly system that will give you maximum output for minimum input.

RAISED BED FRAMES

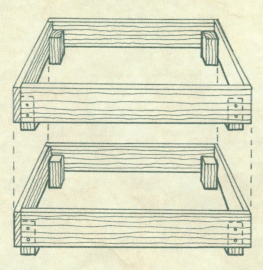

See page 58 for making instructions

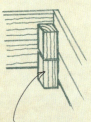

Corner blocks fit together

Advantages of the no-dig system

The no-dig system positively encourages all the elements that are needed in an ideal growing environment. Mulches of garden compost, farm manure and leafmould are all layered in such a way that there is a reduction in pests and diseases, an increase in beneficial soil fungi, worms, insects and microbes, and a decrease in weeds. No-dig draws its inspiration from the natural cycle: vegetation falls to the ground, worms drag the organic matter into the soil, microscopic soil life works on the organic matter, more vegetation falls, and so on.

Minimum weeding

If you allow weeds to seed, you will be faced with many years of weeding. The no-dig system buries the seeds under layers of mulch where they are never given the chance to germinate.

Less effort

Unlike traditional cultivation where you dig the whole plot, and then waste up to half your efforts by walking on and compacting the ground you have painstakingly dug, no-dig raised beds are permanent and never walked on.

MORE BENEFITS OF THE NO-DIG SYSTEM

1   The shape of the beds and paths can be tailored to suit your unique physical needs, whether you have back problems, are in a wheelchair, are partially sighted, dislike bending or just hate digging.

2   You will get higher crop yields on a smaller ground area.

3   It conserves and makes best use of water and organic matter.

4   The structure and make-up of the beds can be targeted to specific plants.

5   The structure of the beds more easily allows the use of physical controls such as nets, windbreaks, plastic sheet or fleece.

CROSS-SECTION OF STACKED RAISED BED FRAMES

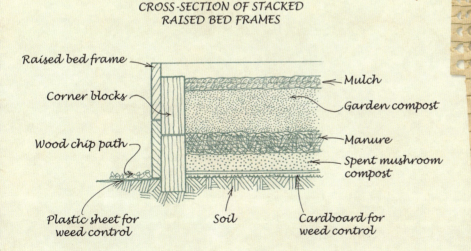

Raised bed frame

Corner blocks

Wood chip path

Plastic sheet for weed control

Mulch

Garden compost

Manure

Spent mushroom compost

Soil

Cardboard for weed control

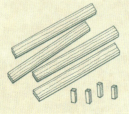

STEP 1

Building raised beds

Raised beds are an essential component of a no-dig garden. They define the growing area, they physically contain the various layers of organic materials and, most importantly, they raise the growing medium above the level of the underlying soil. Beds can be created from just about anything from sawn timber to found containers like baths, dustbins, water tanks and builders' dumpy/jumbo bags.

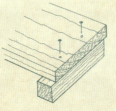

STEP 2

Square module beds

We have designed these beds to be about 90 cm (3 ft) square, so that they can be comfortably reached from all sides, and so that they can be stacked. Make sure, when you are setting out the beds to make paths, that you allow for easy wheelbarrow access.

Building a bed step by step

STEP 1: You need four wooden planks, each 23 cm (9 in) wide, 5 cm (2 in) thick and 90 cm (3 ft) long, and four wooden posts, each 7.5 cm (3 in) square and 23 cm (9 in) long.

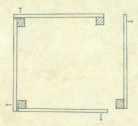

STEP 3

STEP 2: Take a post and screw it to the end of a plank so that it is aligned to the end, and offset to the width by 2.5 cm (1 in).

STEP 3: When you have achieved four identical post-and-plank component parts, screw them together to make the square frame.

STEP 4: Set the frame post-side down on the levelled ground, scrape off any weeds, and then layer the bed up with newspaper and brown card, 5 cm (2 in) compost, 5 cm (2 in) farmyard manure, and 7.5 cm (3 in) spent mushroom compost. See page 57 for how to fill stacked frames.

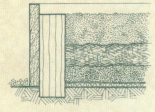

STEP 4

The perfect no-dig garden

Gently sloping to look to the sun at midday, and with a small area of woodland to protect it from the prevailing weather, our no-dig garden has been very carefully considered. We have a polytunnel that gets the sun without casting a shadow over the rest of the plot. On one side of the garden is a wooden shed that is kitted out with pegs for tools, a surface for potting and a couple of old chairs for resting. We have a rabbit-proof fence all around, gates in and out, three compost boxes, plenty of water taps and a bird-proof cage that sits over the fruit beds.

Town garden

A town garden is a good option, as long as all the elements are dedicated to the common no-dig good. I know a couple, with two children, who have replaced the lawns and borders with six raised beds in the front garden and a dozen or so beds and a chicken run in the back. The whole family is enthusiastically involved, the kids with the chickens and the parents with growing food.

Village garden

Another couple, with four children, live in a large end-terrace village house with a huge corner plot that links to a long strip of allotment. They have a pattern of beds and paths that covers the whole garden, six chickens, two beehives, a polytunnel and an old barn. They sell fresh eggs, raw honey and vegetables at the gate – beautiful.

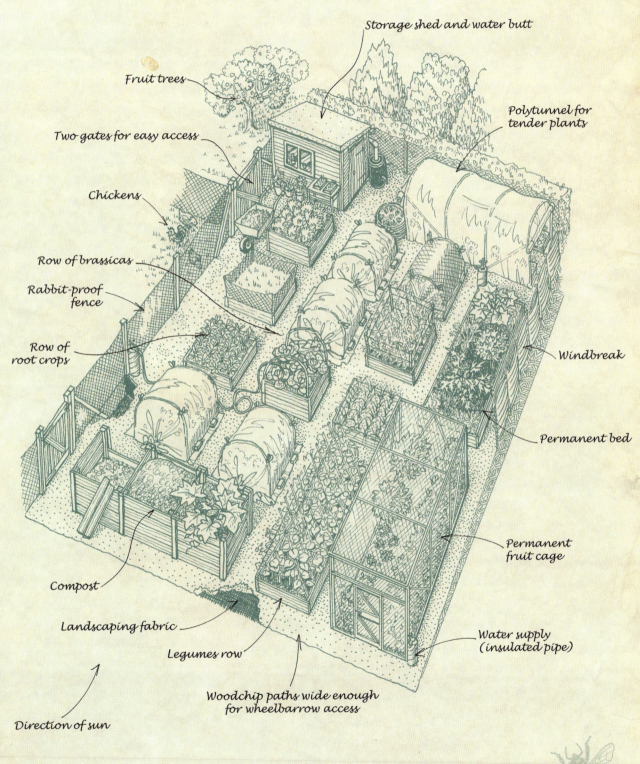

PERFECT NO-DIG PLOT

Fruit trees

Storage shed and water butt

Polytunnel for tender plants

Two gates for easy access

Chickens

Row of brassicas

Rabbit-proof fence

Row of root crops

Windbreak

Permanent bed

Permanent fruit cage

Compost

Landscaping fabric

Legumes row

Water supply (insulated pipe)

Woodchip paths wide enough for wheelbarrow access

Direction of sun

Growing medium
Traditionally, gardeners spent a lifetime of backbreaking effort trying to improve their soil. The no-dig method simply avoids the traditional spade-and-trench slog by layering manure, leafmould and compost in raised beds to create a growing medium that sits on top of the base soil.

Leafmould
Leafmould is a mix of fallen leaves from deciduous shrubs and trees that has been collected and encouraged to decompose speedily. The leaves can be directly added in small amounts to raised beds or stored in compost bins. Once decayed, the leafmould can be added to the beds as a mulch.

Garden compost
Compost is a well-rotted mix of kitchen and garden plant waste and all the leaves and vegetable matter from the garden. We have a group of compost bins on the go, so that vegetable waste can be constantly recycled.

Spent mushroom compost
We use spent mushroom compost as a general, quick-start, weed-stopping mulch when we are looking to top up new beds swiftly. We fill new beds with mushroom compost and then modify them with manure, garden compost or whatever is needed to suit specific crops.

Making a three-bay compost bin
This three-bay bin is much less expensive than making three separate bins. We fill the first bay, and then the second, and then the third. By the time the third bay is being filled, the first is ready to spread on as a mulch. When the first bay is empty, we start to refill it, and so on in a continuous cycle.

THREE-BAY COMPOSTER

Maturing

Removable front planks

Being filled

Being used

Manure

The success of our no-dig vegetable garden set-up – especially the raised beds and the hot beds – is built on manure. Not a pretty picture, maybe, but the size of our crop without fail equates with the amount of manure going in. We use manure from our geese, free horse manure from the local stables, purchased farmyard manure and rabbit manure from a local breeder.

What is well-rotted manure?

Well-rotted farmyard manure is the excrement from livestock like cows, horses and poultry. Manure comes in the form of used bedding. The farmer puts down the bedding (straw or wood shavings), the animals live and excrete on it, and finally the farmer shovels it up and puts it on a heap. Cow, horse and poultry manures are easy to handle and readily available. The best way of getting organic manure is to keep your own livestock.

Keeping geese and using the manure

Our geese are prize-winning manure makers – kitchen scraps, grass, weeds, windfall apples, garden bugs and pests and vegetable garden waste go in, and eggs and 0.5% nitrogen manure come out. We have a lean-to goose house in which we spread straw and shavings. We wait until it is squidgy underfoot, clean it out and leave it to rot, then spread it on the raised beds as mulch.

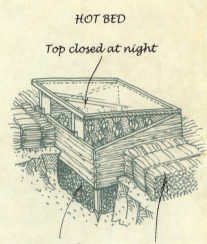

HOT BED

Top closed at night

Buried manure raises temperature

Straw

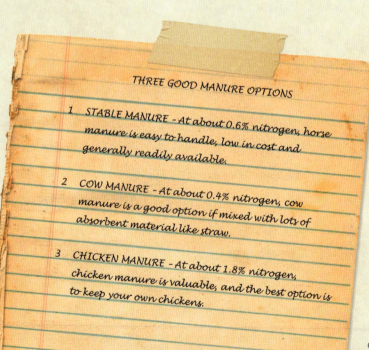

THREE GOOD MANURE OPTIONS

1 STABLE MANURE – At about 0.6% nitrogen, horse manure is easy to handle, low in cost and generally readily available.

2 COW MANURE – At about 0.4% nitrogen, cow manure is a good option if mixed with lots of absorbent material like straw.

3 CHICKEN MANURE – At about 1.8% nitrogen, chicken manure is valuable, and the best option is to keep your own chickens.

Rotation

Generally, if you repeatedly plant the same crops on the same ground, the crops and the ground will become 'sick'. This can be avoided by having a three-year rotation, meaning that you grow, say, brassicas in year one, root vegetables in year two, legumes and salad leaves in year three, and then go back to brassicas in year four.

YEAR 1

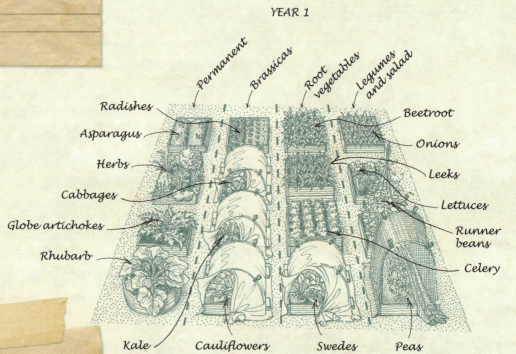

Permanent — Brassicas — Root vegetables — Legumes and salad

Radishes
Asparagus
Herbs
Cabbages
Globe artichokes
Rhubarb

Beetroot
Onions
Leeks
Lettuces
Runner beans
Celery

Kale — Cauliflowers — Swedes — Peas

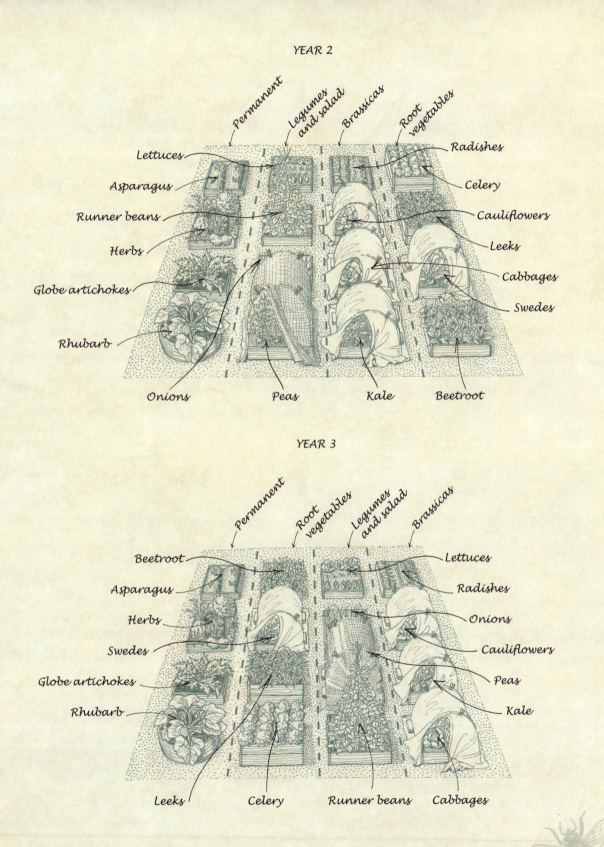

YEAR 2

Permanent

Legumes and salad

Brassicas

Root vegetables

Lettuces

Asparagus

Runner beans

Herbs

Globe artichokes

Rhubarb

Radishes

Celery

Cauliflowers

Leeks

Cabbages

Swedes

Onions

Peas

Kale

Beetroot

YEAR 3

Permanent

Root vegetables

Legumes and salad

Brassicas

Beetroot

Asparagus

Herbs

Swedes

Globe artichokes

Rhubarb

Lettuces

Radishes

Onions

Cauliflowers

Peas

Kale

Leeks

Celery

Runner beans

Cabbages

Year-round calendar
The following calendar will not answer all your questions, but it will give you a general framework and timetable to work to.

MID-WINTER
Inspect your tools; sort out things like stakes, posts, string, pots, plastic sheets, netting and fleece. Set seed potatoes to sprout, order seeds, plan out the pattern of beds, and generally make ready.
- Remove surface weeds, spread mulch, well-rotted manure or garden compost as appropriate, and order seeds.
- Plant broad beans in your chosen beds. Sow extra beans in pots. Sow onions, leeks and radishes in a protected bed or hot bed.
- Pick Brussels sprouts, winter cabbages, last of the carrots, celery, chicory and anything else that is ready.

LATE WINTER
Clean up the paths around the beds and generally make sure that all your gear is in good order. Cover beds at night with fleece and/or nets. Look at your master plan and see if you can get ahead with more mulching.
- Use the hoe and rake to prepare seed beds; look for a nice warm corner and make sure that you have protective screens and fleece at the ready. Remove weeds; maybe add a thin mulch on selected beds, and put debris on the compost heap.
- Plant artichokes and shallots. Sow early peas and maybe another row or two of broad beans. Check crops that have been sown in pots. Sow carrots, lettuces and radishes under glass/plastic/mats on a hot bed. Raise seedlings in warm frames (crops

such as leeks, cucumbers, onions and tomatoes).
- Pick Brussels sprouts, winter cabbages, last of the carrots, celery, chicory and anything else that is ready.

EARLY SPRING
Weed paths, mend frames, keep pulling large weeds. Look at your plot and see if you want to change things around, such as the position of the permanent plot.
- Keep stirring with the hoe and generally be on the lookout for weeds, especially deep-rooted perennials.
- Sow hardy seeds out of doors (lettuces, parsnips). Sow crops like spinach, broccoli, leeks, onions, peas, celery, tomatoes and marrows under glass or in a protected bed, either directly in the bed or in trays.
- Pick Brussels sprouts, cabbages and cauliflowers.

MID-SPRING
Be on the lookout for slugs and snails. Watch out for problems on fruit beds. Thin seedlings as necessary. Keep pulling large weeds and putting down mulches to control surface weeds. Reduce the number of sprouts on seed potatoes. Cover selected beds at night.
- Keep working the beds with the hoe and your hands, along the rows of seedlings. Draw the soil up around potatoes.
- You can now sow just about everything in the open. Plant maincrop potatoes. Plant onions, radishes, maincrop

carrots, beet, salsify and scorzonera, endives, more lettuces, peas and spinach. Plant out any seedlings that you have hardened off – things like Brussels sprouts. Sow runner beans, marrows and courgettes under glass.
- Pick beet leaf and broccoli.

LATE SPRING
Keep a watch on the weather and be ready to protect tender seedlings with glass, plastic sheet, net screens or whatever seems appropriate. Be ready to deal with blackfly on beans. Set twigs among the peas. Put mulch on selected beds. Reduce the number of runners on the strawberries. Water seedlings. Keep on delicately hoeing and weeding.
- Prepare more seed beds. Hoe and rake regularly. Heap the growing medium to protect potatoes. Mulch between rows of more advanced vegetables.
- Plant out hardy seedlings. Sow tender vegetables in vacant beds. Sow beans in the open – French, runners and brown. Sow more peas, endives, radishes and summer spinach – and almost anything that takes your fancy. Plant out Brussels sprouts, broccoli, cucumbers and anything else that suits your needs.
- Pick beet leaf, broccoli, early beetroot, early carrots, cucumbers under cover, endives and other vegetables too numerous to mention.

EARLY SUMMER

Bring in fresh manure, well-rotted manure and spent mushroom compost. Keep everything well watered. Spread mulches around crops such as turnips. Put nets over fruit. Remove weak canes from the raspberries. Clean out empty beds and keep on hoeing and weeding. Stake up runner beans and peas.

- Keep hoeing. Dig up potatoes. Weed and mulch vacant seed beds.
- Plant out seedlings. Sow succession crops like endives, lettuces and radishes.
- Pick anything that takes your fancy.

MID-SUMMER

Support plants that look hot and droopy. Gather soft fruits as needed. Cut mint and herbs ready for drying. Topdress with manure mulch. Look at the tomatoes and pinch out and feed as necessary. Lift potatoes. Keep hoeing between crops. Water and weed. Make sure that the polytunnel/greenhouse and frames are open to the air.

- Weed, hoe and mulch. Weed after lifting potatoes. Earth up around maincrop potatoes.
- Plant out celery and crops like cabbage, Brussels sprouts and broccoli.
- Keep picking, eating and storing.

LATE SUMMER

Order seeds for autumn sowing. Keep storing vegetables for the winter – bottling, drying and freezing. Bend over the necks of onions. Dry herbs. Pinch out the tops of tomatoes. Clear and mulch beds. Protect fruit crops from the birds. Plant out new strawberry beds. Keep hoeing and weeding.

- Weed and hoe. Weed any empty potato beds.
- Make more sowings of endives, radishes, spinach, onions and anything else that fits the season. Sow lettuces and salad crops under cover. Sow cabbages for spring planting.
- Keep picking, eating and storing. Dry more herbs. Gather beans, tomatoes and fruits when they are ready.

EARLY AUTUMN

Watch out for and protect from frosts. Lift and store roots. Earth up celery and leeks. Watch out for and destroy caterpillars. Prune raspberries. Water, weed and hoe as necessary. Blanch endives.

- Weed, hoe and mulch as soon as you have cleared the crops.
- Plant out spring cabbages. Look at your seed packets and sow if possible.
- Lift potatoes and onions. Gather runner beans. Lift and store roots. Gather and store fruit as it ripens. Keep picking and eating other crops as needed.

MID-AUTUMN

Watch out for frost and protect as needed. Mulch vacant beds. Continue hoeing and weeding. Clear the ground and put debris on the compost heap. Clean up paths and maintain beds. Thin onions.

- Weed, hoe and mulch beds as they become vacant.
- Plant rhubarb. Plant fruit trees. Sow peas in a protected beds. Sow salad crops under glass. Plant out seedlings. Sow early peas in warm areas.
- Gather the remaining tomatoes. Lift and pick crops such as celeriac and carrots.

LATE AUTUMN

Watch out for frost and protect as needed. Clean up leaves and debris; weed and mulch vacant beds. Continue hoeing and weeding as necessary. Remove bean and pea sticks and poles.

- Weed, hoe and mulch beds as they become vacant.
- Sow broad beans in a sheltered spot.
- Lift and store root crops. Cut, lift and eat other crops as needed.

EARLY WINTER

Watch out for frosts and protect as needed. Clean the tools and the shed.

- Weed hoe and mulch beds as they become vacant. Check that stored vegetables are in good order.
- If the weather is very mild, plant broad beans. Draw growing medium up around the peas. Sow salad crops under glass and protect as needed.
- Pick the last of the beet leaf. Pick Brussels sprouts, winter cabbages, last of the carrots, celery, chicory and anything else that is ready.

Quick-reference sowing table

The following table gives the sowing times, and the distance between plants, for a wide variety of vegetables. Be aware that the no-dig method allows you to grow more plants in a given area and to lengthen the season by sowing early and cropping later.

ARTICHOKES, GLOBE	Sow mid-spring, 45–90 cm (18–36 in) apart
ARTICHOKES, JERUSALEM	Plant late winter to mid-spring, 25 cm (10 in) apart
ASPARAGUS	Sow early to mid-spring, 45 cm (18 in) apart
AUBERGINES (EGGPLANTS)	Sow early spring, 30–45 cm (12–18 in) apart
BEANS, BROAD	Sow late winter to mid-spring or late autumn, 20–25 cm (8–10 in) apart
BEANS, FRENCH	Sow mid-spring to early summer, 13–15 cm (5–6 in) apart
BEANS, RUNNER	Sow late spring to early summer, 15–20 cm (6–8 in) apart
BEET LEAF	Sow mid- to late spring, 20–25 cm (8–10 in) apart
BEETROOT	Sow early spring to late summer, 10–13 cm (4–5 in) apart
BROCCOLI	Sow mid- to late spring, 30–45 cm (12–18 in) apart
BRUSSELS SPROUTS	Sow early to mid-spring, 45–90 cm (18–36 in) apart
CABBAGES	Sow spring varieties mid- to late summer, summer varieties late winter to late spring, winter varieties early to late spring, all 30 cm (12 in) apart
CAPSICUMS (SWEET PEPPERS)	Sow late winter to early spring, 30–45 cm (12–18 in) apart
CARROTS	Sow early spring to early summer, 5–7.5 cm (2–3 in) apart
CAULIFLOWERS	Sow early to late spring, 30–45 cm (12–18 in) apart
CELERIAC	Sow early to mid-spring, plant out late spring to early summer, 25 cm (10 in) apart
CELERY	Sow early to mid-spring under glass, plant out late spring to early summer 23–30 cm (9–12 in) apart
CHICORY	Sow late spring to mid-summer, 20 cm (8 in) apart
CUCUMBERS, OUTDOOR RIDGE TYPE	Sow mid- to late spring, plant out 45 cm (18 in) apart

GARLIC	Plant out autumn to early spring, 15–25 cm (6–10 in) apart
KALE	Sow mid- to late spring, plant out early to late summer, 38–45 cm (15–18 in) apart
LAND CRESS	For autumn to spring crop sow mid- to late summer, for summer crop sow spring to early summer, 20–25 cm (8–10 in) apart
LEEKS	Sow mid- to late winter or early to mid-spring, plant out mid-summer 15–20 cm (6–8 in) apart
LETTUCES	Sow spring varieties late summer to mid-autumn, summer varieties early spring to mid-summer, 20–35 cm (8–10 in) apart
MARROWS AND COURGETTES	Sow mid- to late spring, plant out late spring to early summer one plant to a 90 cm (3 ft) square
ONIONS	Sow early to late spring, 5–15 cm (2–6 in) apart
PARSNIPS	Sow late winter to mid-spring, 13–15 cm (5–6 in) apart
PEAS	Sow early spring to mid-summer, 13–15 cm (5–6 in) apart
RADISHES	Sow mid-winter to early spring, 5–7.5 cm (1–2 in) apart
SPINACH, SUMMER	Sow late winter to late summer, 23–30 cm (9–12 in) apart
SPINACH, WINTER	Sow mid-winter to early summer, 15 cm (6 in) apart
SWEDES	Sow mid-spring to mid-summer, 15–23 cm (6–9 in) apart
SWEETCORN	Sow mid-spring in peat pots, and plant out in late spring 30–40 cm (12–16 in) apart
TOMATOES, INDOORS	Sow late winter to early spring, 60 cm (2 ft) apart
TOMATOES, OUTDOORS	Sow early spring to late spring, 45 cm (18 in) apart
TURNIPS	Sow mid-spring to late summer, 15–23 cm (6–9 in) apart

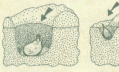

Shallow   Dibber
dug hole   hole

Trench drill

Shallow
v-section drill

Sowing, potting and planting Our

sowing method depends on the type of seeds, the time of year, and our experience the previous time. For example, the other year we had such a mess-up with our peas – the birds and mice took the lot – that we decided always to sow them in plastic gutters full of growing compost in the greenhouse, and then slide the plants into place in the beds when they were well rooted. It works.

Where and how we sow seeds

The raised bed method is so focused, and the seeds so expensive, that we now either (1) sow single seeds or a tiny pinch of seeds directly in shallow dibbed holes or spaced in drills in the beds, and then either thin out to leave a single best plant at each station or lift and replant; or (2) sow in individual pots in the greenhouse/polytunnel and then plant out.

Sowing in the beds

TRENCH DRILL Make a wide, shallow drill and dribble, trail or spot sow single seeds.

V-SECTION DRILL Make a V-section drill and place each seed by hand.

ONIONS – Make a shallow hole and set onion sets in place.

POTATOES – Dig a shallow hole and position individual seed potatoes.

Sowing seeds in trays

1 Cover the drainage holes with broken crocks, fill the tray with moist growing medium, and firm down with a wooden board.

2 Use your palm or a folded piece of paper to gently distribute the seeds.

3 Use a sieve to cover the seeds with a sprinkling of compost.

SOWING SEEDS IN TRAYS

1   2   3

Sowing peas in lengths of plastic gutter

Cut plastic gutter to lengths to suit the width of your raised bed – say 90 cm (3 ft). Tape the ends up with gaffer tape. Fill the gutter with growing medium and sow your peas. When the plants are established, slide the whole thing into the prepared bed and water generously.

Potting on

When some seedlings are large enough to handle, they can be lifted, thinned and transferred to another tray, pot or position that has a greater depth of growing medium.

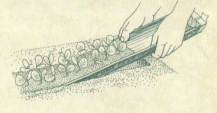

*SOWING IN A
LENGTH OF GUTTER*

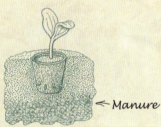

*PLANTING OUT
A PEAT POT*

Manure

*Many seeds can be
nurtured in pots in a
protected environment
and then planted out*

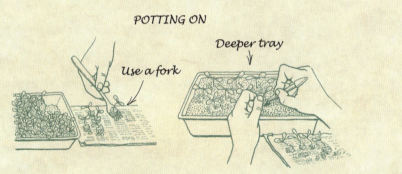

POTTING ON

Use a fork

Deeper tray

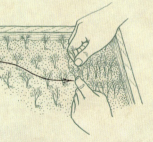

THINNING

*Press down
disturbed soil*

*Some seedlings need to
be thinned out to give
few plants more space*

TRANSPLANTING

*Some seedlings
can be lifted and
transplanted
into their final
growing space in
the bed*

Brassicas

SPROUTING BROCCOLI

Sprouting broccoli – white and purple – can, with a break in early summer, be harvested from early spring to early autumn. Home-grown broccoli is sweet, tender and tasty. Sow mid–late spring and plant early–mid-summer.

Troubleshooting

CATERPILLARS, BUTTERFLIES AND PIGEONS Protect the plants with fleece or fine nets.

DISTORTED LEAVES Aphid and whitefly damage; spray with a solution of water and soap liquid.

Sow seeds thinly in rows 6 mm (¼ in) deep, 15 cm (6 in) apart; keep well watered and thin to 5 cm (2 in) apart

Plant out in dibbed holes 30-45 cm (12-18 in) apart when 13 cm (5 in) high, water and protect with fleece

Harvest: In the following spring, cut centre heads first, then every few days cut sideshoots

Remove dying leaves

Water the seedlings before and after planting

Add another thin mulch of well-rotted compost when the plants are well established

BRUSSELS SPROUTS

Sprouts can be picked from early autumn to early spring. They are at their best when they are very lightly steamed and served with splash of olive oil and a shake of black pepper – but they have to be fresh and they must not be boiled or overcooked. Sow early–mid-spring and plant late spring to early summer.

Troubleshooting

BIRD AND INSECT DAMAGE TO LEAVES Protect the plants with draped nets.

STICKY, DISTORTED LEAVES Aphid damage; remove damaged leaves, spray with a soap liquid solution, and remove and burn the top 2.5 cm (1 in) of the growing medium.

DISTORTED ROOTS AND STUNTED GROWTH Probably clubroot; pull and burn the plants, and plant the next crop at the other end of the garden.

Plant out in dibbed holes 30-45 cm (12-18 in) apart when 15 cm (6 in) high and firm around the base

In windy areas, stake and put up protection

Thin to 5 cm (2 in) apart when 2.5 cm (1 in) high, and water well

Remove yellow leaves

Sow in seed bed 6 mm (¼ in) deep in rows 25 cm (10 in) apart

Draw medium up to the stem base, firm up and mulch

Sow seeds thinly
in a seed bed
18 mm (¾ in)
deep, 15 cm
(6 in) apart

Dib holes
30 cm (1 ft)
apart

Draw up
the medium
around the
stems and
remove dead
leaves

Thin to
5 cm (2 in)
apart

Protect from root fly with a
collar around the base; also
cover with fleece to guard
against butterfly attack

CABBAGES

Cabbages provide a year-round supply. Spring cabbage:
sow mid–late summer, plant early–mid autumn and
harvest mid–late spring. Summer cabbage: sow early–mid
spring, plant late spring–early summer and harvest late
summer–early autumn. Winter cabbage: sow mid–late
spring, plant mid-summer and harvest late winter.

Troubleshooting

ROOT FLY Seen as rotting stumps and blotchy foliage;
place a felt, plastic or carpet collar around the plant to
keep off the egg-laying flies.
MOULD Spray the plants with an organic anti-mould mix.
APHID Spray with a water and soap solution, burn the top
2.5 cm (1 in) of growing medium and burn the plants at
the end of the season.
HOLES IN LEAVES Caused by caterpillars and birds; avoid
the problem by growing in a netted cage.
DISTORTED ROOT AND POOR GROWTH Probably clubroot;
pull and burn the plants and rotate crops.

Puddle 13 cm
(5 in) high
seedlings into
dibbed holes
30-45 cm
(12-18 in) apart
and fit collars

When curds
form, protect by
snapping two
large leaves as
a cover

Sow thinly
12 mm (½ in)
deep, with
20 cm (8 in)
between rows

Mulch

Note: Protect
with fleece or
fine net against
caterpillar
damage

CAULIFLOWERS

Cauliflowers can be cut in mid-summer and early autumn
to the following early summer. They can be a challenge to
grow, but it is well worth a try. That said, if you enjoy the
taste and texture of cauliflower but have tried and failed,
a good, easier-to-grow alternative is calabrese (a variety of
broccoli). Sow mid-spring and plant early summer.

Troubleshooting

LEAF SPOT Shows as rusty brown spots on the leaves; if
the crop fails, burn the plants and move to another bed
next time.
MEALY APHID Shows as sticky blue-grey colonies on the
underside of leaves; spray with a water and soap solution,
remove and burn the top 2.5 cm (1 in) of growing
medium and burn the plants at the end of the season.
BIRD AND INSECT HOLES IN LEAVES Avoid the problem by
building a fine-net cage over the crop.

KALE

Kale (also called borecole and curly kale) figures highly in our scheme of things as we all enjoy it – Gill and I eat the young tender shoots and leaves, and the geese make a mad scramble for the rest. Sow late spring to early summer, plant mid-summer and harvest late autumn to mid-spring (first eat the crown and then the sideshoots).

Troubleshooting

MEALY APHIDS Shows as sticky aphids on the underside of leaves; spray off with a water and soap solution, remove and burn the top 2.5 cm (1 in) of growing medium and burn the plants and debris at the end of the season.

POOR GROWTH, YELLOW LEAVES Probably caused by wind rock; support the plants with sticks.

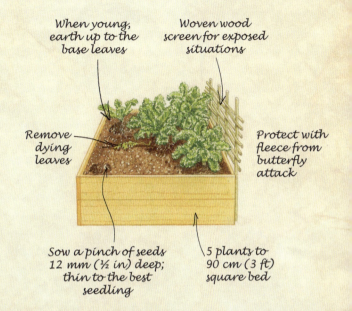

When young, earth up to the base leaves

Woven wood screen for exposed situations

Remove dying leaves

Protect with fleece from butterfly attack

Sow a pinch of seeds 12 mm (½ in) deep; thin to the best seedling

5 plants to 90 cm (3 ft) square bed

Thin to strongest seedlings

Remove damaged leaves when they appear

Plant 3–4 seeds at 23 cm (9 in) intervals

Add more mulch as the plants reach maturity

Salad leaves

BEET LEAF

Beet leaf (also known as spinach beet, perpetual spinach and chard) can be harvested from mid-summer around to the following summer. If you find spinach a bit difficult to grow and are prepared to try a slightly tougher and stronger-flavoured alternative, this is a good option. Sow mid-spring to late summer.

Troubleshooting

BOLTING Caused by lack of water; water generously.
TOUGH EATING Pick when the leaves are small.

Pinch of seeds 12 mm (½ in) deep, 20 cm (8 in) apart, and thin to best plant

Store in dry sand

In spring plant four roots in a pot of compost and cover with black plastic

In autumn, use fork to lift the mature plant

Trim leaves 2.5 cm (1 in) from crown

Trim roots

CHICORY

Although chicory is tricky to grow, the fact that it can be harvested right through winter when other salad crops are thin on the ground makes it a great option. Chicory makes a perfect lunch snack with brown bread, olive oil, a strong onion and a sprinkling of cheese. Sow early summer and harvest autumn to spring.

Troubleshooting

SLUGS A real pest; remove by hand.
HEART ROT Shows as yellow-brown damage; protect from frost and/or use a different variety next time.

LAND CRESS AND OTHER SALAD LEAVES

Land cress, curled cress, rocket, lamb's lettuce and other leaves can be harvested from late autumn to early winter and from spring onwards. For the perfect lunchtime treat, take a handful of leaves, a chunk of home-made brown bread and a crunchy apple. Sow late spring to early summer.

Troubleshooting

SLUGS AND SNAILS A real pest; keep removing by hand.
BROWN TIRED LEAVES The plants need watering.

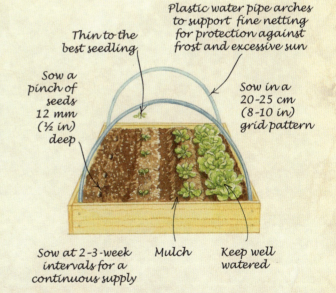

Plant seeds 6 mm (¼ in) deep in a 15–20 cm (6–8 in) grid pattern

Pinch out to leave best seedlings

Mulch

Harvest young leaves to encourage new growth

Well-rotted manure and compost layers

Cover with fine netting to guard against flea beetle; water well

---

LETTUCES

When I was a kid, we had lettuces that were either round or long, and that was it. Now we have every shape, texture and taste imaginable. For children, a good starting point is to serve it up with fresh bread, soft goat's cheese and a creamy dip – they will love it. Summer varieties: sow late spring and harvest mid–late summer. Spring varieties: sow early autumn and harvest mid–late spring.

Troubleshooting

SLUGS AND SNAILS A real pest; remove by hand.
APHIDS Seen as sticky damage; spray with liquid soap solution, then remove and burn the debris.

Plastic water pipe arches to support fine netting for protection against frost and excessive sun

Thin to the best seedling

Sow a pinch of seeds 12 mm (½ in) deep

Sow in a 20–25 cm (8–10 in) grid pattern

Sow at 2–3-week intervals for a continuous supply

Mulch

Keep well watered

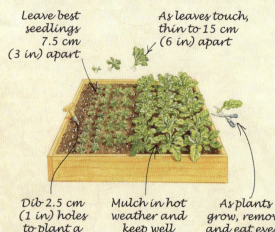

Leave best seedlings 7.5 cm (3 in) apart

As leaves touch, thin to 15 cm (6 in) apart

Dib 2.5 cm (1 in) holes to plant a pinch of seeds

Mulch in hot weather and keep well watered

As plants grow, remove and eat every other row

SPINACH

If you choose a range of varieties and offer protection throughout the growing period, you can pick spinach for most of the year. It is great steamed and served up with new potatoes, but best of all when picked as baby leaves and eaten raw in a sandwich. Sow mid-spring.

Troubleshooting

DISTORTED GROWTH Pull out anything that looks sick.
TIRED GROWTH Have several beds on the go, and remove tired plants.

Stalks and shoots

GLOBE ARTICHOKES

Although the globe artichoke is a perennial, it is one of those plants that can be left in place in the same bed. They are something of an acquired taste, but the great big, spiked, purple flowers are stunning! Sow late spring, plant early summer and harvest early–mid-autumn.

Troubleshooting

SLUGS Remove slugs as soon as they appear.
INSECT ATTACK Spray with a liquid soap solution.
RUST Caused by a fungus; burn affected plants.

Plant suckers 10 cm (4 in) deep

Harvest: Cut while scales are closed and leave 5 cm (2 in) stem

Well-rotted manure

In spring and autumn mulch with dung

ASPARAGUS

Asparagus is not difficult to grow, but time-consuming – you might have to wait 3–4 years before you get a good crop. That said, once the plants are established you can expect them to crop for 20 years or more. Sow and plant in mid-spring. In years 2–3, harvest in late spring.

Troubleshooting

SLUGS A real pest; remove them by hand.
NEW PLANT FAILURE Burn the crop and try again on a new bed.
FROST Spread a thick straw mulch to protect from frost.

Crowns 45 cm (18 in) apart covered by 5–7.5 cm (2–3 in) compost (add more as the plant grows)

Each autumn, cut foliage away before berries ripen

Thin mulch of rotted manure

25 x 38 cm (10 x 15 in) trench

Fill base with 7.5 cm (3 in) mound of compost

Cut spears 7.5-10 cm (3-4 in) below ground

Sow 12 mm
(½ in) deep

Keep warm
and well
watered

When 30 cm
(1 ft) high,
tie and add
compost up to
lower leaves;
continue as
plant grows

Protect with
straw in
icy winter
weather

Plant in
individual
7.5 cm (3 in)
peat pots

Manure
topped with
compost

Add extra
frames as
plants grow

CELERY

I once thought that growing celery was a challenge,
but growing it in raised beds is relatively straightforward.
A freshly picked celery stick with bread and cheese cannot
be beaten. Sow early–mid-spring, plant early summer and
harvest late autumn.

Troubleshooting

SLUGS AND SNAILS A real pest; remove them by hand.
BROWN/WET ROTS Avoid the problem by protecting from
frost and waterlogged soil.

Seeds and pods

BROAD BEANS

Broad beans are hardy, they can be densely planted, they give a high plant-to-space return, they can be stored by drying or freezing, and they taste good. Sow summer crop in mid-spring and harvest late summer; sow winter crop in late autumn and harvest in early summer.

Troubleshooting

WIND DAMAGE Avoid the problem by supporting the crop with sticks and binding around with strings, so that the entire contents of the bed are supported.

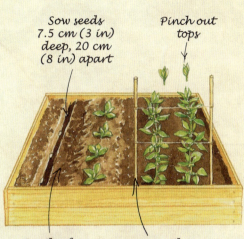

Sow seeds 7.5 cm (3 in) deep, 20 cm (8 in) apart

Pinch out tops

Depth of soil 45 cm (18 in)

Support with sticks and strings

FRENCH BEANS

More tender than runner beans but perhaps less tasty, French beans are well worth planting because they can be cropped two or three weeks before runner beans. Sow late spring and harvest late summer.

Troubleshooting

WIND DAMAGE Avoid the problem by supporting the crop with sticks and binding around with strings, so that the entire contents of the bed are supported.

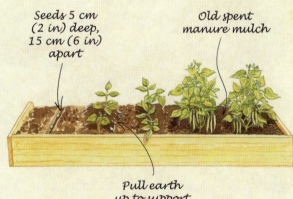

Seeds 5 cm (2 in) deep, 15 cm (6 in) apart

Old spent manure mulch

Pull earth up to support young plants

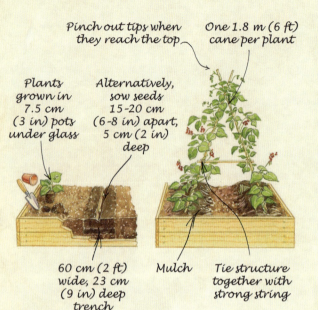

Pinch out tips when they reach the top

One 1.8 m (6 ft) cane per plant

Plants grown in 7.5 cm (3 in) pots under glass

Alternatively, sow seeds 15-20 cm (6-8 in) apart, 5 cm (2 in) deep

60 cm (2 ft) wide, 23 cm (9 in) deep trench

Mulch

Tie structure together with strong string

RUNNER BEANS

If I could only grow one crop, it would be runner beans. I enjoy the whole experience of sowing, planting, building the support frames, eating mountains of fresh beans, freezing, salting, the pleasure of giving gluts to friends, neighbours and the geese. Sow late spring to early summer and harvest mid-summer to mid-autumn.

Troubleshooting

DAMAGE TO YOUNG PLANTS We have a two-pronged approach: we sow beans directly in the beds and we also grow beans in pots in the greenhouse, so that we can fill in if plants fail.

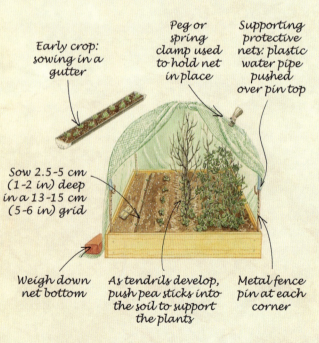

Early crop: sowing in a gutter

Peg or spring clamp used to hold net in place

Supporting protective nets: plastic water pipe pushed over pin top

Sow 2.5-5 cm (1-2 in) deep in a 13-15 cm (5-6 in) grid

Weigh down net bottom

As tendrils develop, push pea sticks into the soil to support the plants

Metal fence pin at each corner

PEAS

Peas are all good, although they can be tricky because birds and mice eat them at the sowing stage. We have solved this problem by sowing them in lengths of plastic gutter in the greenhouse and then sliding the strips of plants into place in the bed. Sow mid–late spring and harvest early summer to mid–autumn.

Troubleshooting

MICE A real nuisance; sow as described above and protect the crop with nets, fleece and traps.
MOULD AND MILDEW Shows as white patchy leaves; water generously and drench with an organic spray.

SWEETCORN

When I was a kid in the late 1950s, 'Exotic Sweet Tasting Miracle Indian Corn' was all the rage – the sort of thing that you grew if you were adventurous. Now, although sweetcorn is still something of a miracle and it tastes better than ever, it is grown as a maincrop. Sow late spring and harvest late summer to early autumn.

Troubleshooting

MICE A pest at every stage; we use traps and little windmills to deter them.

LIMP LEAVES Increase the watering.

One seed 2.5 cm (1 in) deep per peat pot under glass

Mature plants reach over 1.5 m (5 ft) high

Plant in a grid 30 cm (1 ft) apart

Plant out at the five-leaf stage

Heap mulch around base

Onions and relatives

ONIONS AND SHALLOTS

If, like us, you eat onions just about every day – in stews, soups, salads, sandwiches, pickles, chutneys and so on – then you need to grow as many types and forms as possible. We sow seeds, plant sets, sow spring and summer varieties – anything to increase our total crop. From sets: sow early spring and harvest late summer. Spring sowing from seed for summer: sow early spring and harvest late summer. Summer sowing from seed to overwinter: sow late summer and harvest late summer the following year.

Troubleshooting

MAGGOTY BULBS Pull and burn.

DARK GREEN, DROOPING LEAVES Indicate too much nitrogen; use a sandy medium next time.

Thin out seedlings in stages

Plant seedlings on a 7.5-10 cm (3-4 in) grid; pull soil away from bulb

Uproot in sunny conditions to dry on nets, with roots facing the sun

Sow seeds 6 mm (¼ in) deep very thinly

Water seedling into 2.5 cm (1 in) hole and firm sides

Trim tips and roots before planting

Net stretched over supporting canes secured by string and pegs

LEEKS

If you are looking for an onion-type crop that you can more or less leave in over winter, leeks are the answer. We grow ours in the bottom of very deep frames so that we can add extra mulch little by little, so all but the tops of the plants are covered. Sow early–mid-spring, plant early–mid-summer and harvest mid-winter.

Troubleshooting

SAGGING STEMS Suggest that the stems need support; earth them up to a greater depth.

SLIMY STEMS IN WINTER Provide more frost protection.

Dib 15 cm (6 in) deep holes at 15-20 cm (6-8 in) intervals

Mulch when established and build up the soil

Drop in the seedling and water in

Frame added as plants grow

GARLIC

Not so long ago, garlic was only used in minuscule amounts, but now it is used just about everywhere. My sure-fire winter cold cure-all is: three cloves of garlic chopped and sprinkled on a slice of toast, all drenched with olive oil, and eaten just like that for breakfast and supper. Plant early spring and harvest late summer.

Troubleshooting

BIRDS Can be a real pest at the planting stage; keep them off with a fine net.
BOLTING Conditions are too extreme; avoid too much water, shade or drought.

Cover developing plants to prevent birds pecking them up

Spring clamps or pegs and sticks laid across support the net

Plant single cloves 10-15 cm (4-6 in) deep and 15-20 cm (6-8 in) apart

Fork up the bulb and leave in sun to dry

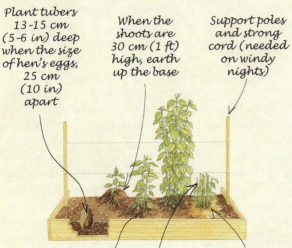

Plant tubers 13–15 cm (5–6 in) deep when the size of hen's eggs, 25 cm (10 in) apart

When the shoots are 30 cm (1 ft) high, earth up the base

Support poles and strong cord (needed on windy nights)

When 60 cm (2 ft) high, apply extra mulch to form 15 cm (6 in) mound

Cut down stems to 30 cm (1 ft) high

Chopped straw mulch to protect tubers from frost until needed

Roots and tubers

JERUSALEM ARTICHOKES

Jerusalem artichokes (also called sunchokes and sunroots) are very easy to grow. Last year we planted four square beds each with five tubers, and now we have 20 enormous plants. One plant gives us a bucket of tubers. As for eating, think of a soft, sweet, chestnutty potato. Plant early spring and harvest mid–late autumn.

Troubleshooting

SLUGS Can be a nuisance at the early leafing stage; remove by hand.

TROUBLESOME TUBERS As even the smallest tuber will grow, leave the crop in the same bed year after year.

BEETROOT

Beetroot figures highly in our self-sufficiency scheme. It is beautifully easy to grow, it tastes great hot or cold, it can be stored as a root in a cold shed, it can be frozen as a soup-mush mix and it can be pickled in sugar or vinegar or turned into a chutney or jam. Sow late spring and harvest late summer.

Troubleshooting

SLUGS Can be a pest at all stages; remove them by hand.
BOLTING AND SPLITTING ROOTS Both problems are caused by lack of water; add mulch and water generously.

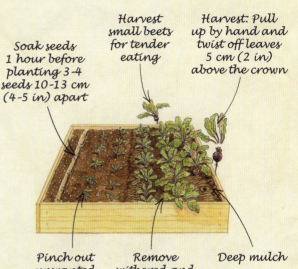

Soak seeds 1 hour before planting 3-4 seeds 10-13 cm (4-5 in) apart

Harvest small beets for tender eating

Harvest: Pull up by hand and twist off leaves 5 cm (2 in) above the crown

Pinch out unwanted seedlings

Remove withered and dead leaves

Deep mulch

CARROTS

Carrots are a good all-rounder. They are relatively easy to grow, they are good on the eye, they taste and smell good, they can be cooked or eaten raw, they can be stored as roots, they can be used variously in pickles and chutneys, they have a long growing season, and even 'don't like veg' kids will eat them because they are sweet. Sow mid–late spring and harvest mid-summer to mid-autumn.

Troubleshooting

SOGGY HOLES IN ROOTS Could be slugs or carrot fly; treat for fly as shown and pick off slugs.
GREEN TOP Prevent by earthing up to keep the sunlight off the shoulders.

Plant seeds very thinly 18 mm (¾ in) deep, with 13-15 cm (5-6 in) between the rows

Protect the growing carrots from carrot fly with a 90 cm (3 ft) net or plastic barrier all around the bed

Thin to 5 cm (2 in) apart in the evening

Pull up soil around plants

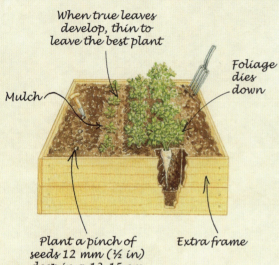

When true leaves
develop, thin to
leave the best plant

Foliage
dies
down

Mulch

Plant a pinch of
seeds 12 mm (½ in)
deep in a 13-15 cm
(5-6 in) grid pattern

Extra frame

PARSNIPS

When I was a kid staying in the country with my
grandparents, we ate parsnips that were boiled, roast,
mashed with cream, hashed with meat, and cooked and
served up in just about every way you can imagine – and
very nice they were too. If you do not have much luck
growing potatoes, then perhaps parsnips would be the
answer. Sow early spring and harvest early–mid-winter.

Troubleshooting

FANGING OR FORKING Caused by over-fresh manure
and/or stones; avoid the problem next time.
CANKER Shows as a brown mess around the shoulders
and is caused by slugs or physical damage; remove slugs
and earth up to protect the roots.

Chitting:
tubers should be
rose end up

Every 2-3
weeks, draw up
the medium
around the
shoots

Use a fork
to draw the
tubers up to
the surface

Dig 15 cm (6 in) deep
holes; plant seed potatoes
with 2.5 cm (1 in) long
shoots uppermost

Add frames
to build up
depth as the
plants grow

POTATOES

Whereas Gill and I once grew enough spuds for the whole
year, we now buy about two-thirds of our potatoes in bulk
from the local organic farmer – they are high-quality and
low-cost – and save our valuable space, time and effort for
growing a few special heirloom varieties in near-organic
conditions. Plant mid-spring and harvest late summer.

Troubleshooting

GREEN POTATOES Caused by potatoes pushing through
the soil and being exposed to sunlight; avoid the problem
by spreading a generous mulch of spent manure around
the plants.
DAMAGED POTATOES When you lift the crop, always eat
the damaged ones first.

RADISHES

Gill and I do not do much forward thinking when it comes to radishes – we just use them as a quick-growing crop for filling in odd spaces. So, if a bed is between crops, or we want something fast-growing, or we simply want more salad, we opt for radishes. All that said, however, they are very tasty! Sow early–mid-spring and harvest early summer to autumn.

Troubleshooting

SLUGS AND SNAILS Always a pest; remove them by hand.
ALL FOLIAGE AND NOT MUCH RADISH Caused by using fresh manure; use well-rotted manure next time.

Thin to 2.5 cm (1 in) apart

Sow in succession every two weeks

Sow 12 mm (½ in) deep in rows 10–15 cm (4–6 in) apart

Mulch in dry weather

Swede sproutings: in mid-winter, keep box in semi-darkness in frost-free shed

Thin to leave strongest plant

Cover with a fleece to guard against butterfly attack

Sow a pinch of seeds in 12 mm (½ in) deep holes every 23 cm (9 in)

Cover with polythene during wet, cold spells

SWEDES

If you have trouble growing potatoes, and if you have the space, then swedes are a good option. A good recipe, much favoured by wartime pilots (and by me and my grandpa) is steamed swedes mashed with cream, sprinkled with salt and pepper, and topped off with a couple of fried eggs, with brown bread and butter on the side. Sow late spring and harvest early winter.

Troubleshooting

SLUGS AND SNAILS Can be a real pest; remove by hand.
BIG FOLIAGE, LITTLE ROOTS This indicates too much nitrogen, meaning an over-rich manure; only use well-rotted manure.

Thin to leave the strongest plant

Winter varieties: harvest young leaves in early summer to eat as greens

Dib 12 mm (½ in) deep holes every 15-20 cm (6-8 in)

In cold areas store in sand in trays in a frost-free place

Inspect under fleece regularly and remove dead leaves

TURNIPS

Forget any bad memories you may have from your school-dinner days, when turnips were as big as cannon balls, woody and disgusting. The small, modern, tender varieties are soft, white, tasty and an all-round delight. Sow early summer and harvest late autumn.

Troubleshooting

SLUGS AND SNAILS Remove by hand.

CELERIAC

If, like us, you enjoy conjuring up new winter salad mixes – including say white cabbage, onions, nuts, celery and sunflower seeds, all chopped up and mixed with olive oil – then you are going to like celeriac. Sow early spring, plant early summer and harvest early winter.

Troubleshooting

SPLITTING Caused by alternate wet-dry conditions; spread mulch of spent manure to hold in the moisture.
SLUGS A real pest; remove by hand.

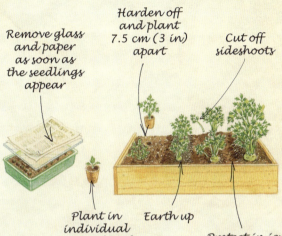

Remove glass and paper as soon as the seedlings appear

Harden off and plant 7.5 cm (3 in) apart

Cut off sideshoots

Plant in individual 7.5 cm (3 in) peat pots

Earth up

Protect in icy winter weather

Fruiting vegetables

AUBERGINES (EGGPLANTS)

Part of the fun of growing aubergines is their shape. One moment the plant is all leaves and the next peeping out of the foliage there are the most extraordinary pendulous purple fruits. We chop them with onions and tomatoes, give the mix a swift stir-fry, eat half, and freeze the rest for another day. Sow early spring, plant mid–late spring and harvest late summer to early autumn.

Troubleshooting

SPLITTING FRUIT Caused by lack of water; increase the watering frequency.

When 30 cm (1 ft) high, support and remove the growing tip

Remove unwanted fruits/flowers to keep 5-6 of the best

Protective screen supports for the plastic or netting to prevent wind damage

Remove glass and paper as soon as the seedlings appear

Plant on in individual 7.5 cm (3 in) pots

In mid- to late spring, plant in the bed

Mulch of well-rotted manure

CAPSICUMS (SWEET PEPPERS)

If you have success growing tomatoes, aubergines and cucumbers, you are probably going to enjoy growing capsicums. We grow lots and eat them in stir-fries and chopped salads. When we have gluts, we add them to tomatoes, apples and onions and make chutney. Sow early spring, plant late spring and harvest late summer.

Troubleshooting

ROLLED LEAVES This suggests that the plant is too cold; increase protection.
MOULD Caused by a virus; spray with a soap solution and, if things worsen, spray with an organic anti-mould drench.

Remove glass and paper as soon as the seedlings appear

Plant out when all risk of frost has passed; pinch out growing point and support with a cane

Plastic for wind protection

Plant in individual 7.5 cm (3 in) peat pots

Extra frame if gales are forecast

CUCUMBERS
(OUTDOOR RIDGE TYPE)

We grow our outdoor ridge cucumbers in much the same way as we grow courgettes. We fill a deep bed with a good depth of fresh manure topped with well-rotted manure, start the plants off in the greenhouse, and plant them out when the stems are slightly hairy. Outdoors: sow late spring, plant early summer and harvest late summer. Indoors: sow mid-spring, plant late spring and harvest mid–late summer.

Troubleshooting

SLUGS Can be a big pest at the just-planted stage; remove the slugs daily until the plant stems are stout and hairy.

Sow 2–3 seeds 18 mm (¾ in) deep in 7.5 cm (3 in) pots

Plant out when true leaves appear; nip out growing point after 5–6 leaves

Spring clamp or peg

Plastic water pipe and polythene protection

Cover

Choose the best seedlings and discard the others

Spread out the laterals as they grow; stop them when they reach the sides

MARROWS AND COURGETTES

We grow mountains of courgettes and marrows. We enjoy stuffed marrow with roast potatoes, fried baby courgettes on toast, pickled courgettes in sweet vinegar, marrow and ginger jam, marrow and onion chutney, and vast quantities of a marrow and onion mess that we stir-fry and freeze. Sow mid-spring, plant late spring and harvest late summer.

Troubleshooting

SLUGS A terrible pest at the just-planted stage; we find that the plants are safe from attack when the stems become hairy.

HARVESTING Keep picking when young to encourage more growth.

Fleece used at start of the season to protect against frost

Plastic water pipe arches will support a protective cover for windy areas

Sow two seeds 18 mm (¾ in) deep in peat pots; pinch out to leave the best seedling

Plant out in peat pots when stems become hairy

Pinch out end of leader when it reaches the side

Extra frame

Cover with newspaper and glass until the shoots appear

When big enough to handle, plant in 7.5 cm (3 in) peat pots

Pinch out and stop

Two leaves above last truss

Four trusses only

Support ties every 30 cm (1 ft)

Protect from cold winds

Remove sideshoots on cordon varieties

1.5 m (5 ft) bamboo cane support

Plant 45 cm (18 in) apart

TOMATOES (OUTDOOR)

We grow tomatoes not to eat fresh – although fresh tomatoes are great – but to mix with other things for winter eating. We dry them, stir-fry with onions and peppers and freeze, make ketchup, chutney and pickles… anything to raise our winter spirits. Sow early–mid-spring, plant late spring and harvest late summer to early autumn.

Troubleshooting

MOULDS AND MILDEW Remove damaged foliage as soon as it yellows, and spray with an organic anti-mould drench if the problem looks to be getting out of hand.

Herbs and self-sufficiency
Herbs are plants that are valued for their flavour, scent or healing qualities, and they figure highly in our self-sufficient scheme. Although primarily we use them in cooking, in a small way we also use them as safe and effective healing therapies, and as plant sprays and drenches. For example, while we use mint in a sauce to pour on roast potatoes, we also use it as a medicinal tea to ease indigestion, as a mix for scenting baths and as a drench in the garden.

Getting started
Start with familiar items that you already know how to grow and use, and then go for the unknowns when time allows. Plant in dedicated beds so that you can shape the growing medium to suit the specific needs of each herb, and control the spread of the ones with a more invasive habit.

BAY (SWEET BAY)
A hardy, evergreen shrub with dark green, aromatic leaves that grows to a height of 1.8–3.5 m (6–12 ft) and likes a well-drained, moisture-retentive medium in a sunny position. We use the leaves to give flavour to stews and fish dishes. Used traditionally by herbalists for nerves, aches, sore eyes and bruises.

BORAGE
A hardy annual with oval, slightly hairy, green leaves that grows to a height of about 90 cm (3 ft) and likes a well-drained, moisture-retentive medium in full sun. We use the leaves in cold drinks and salads. Used traditionally by herbalists to increase perspiration, as a mild sedative and as a wash for soothing various skin conditions.

CHERVIL
A hardy biennial that is usually grown as an annual, with bright green, fern-like leaves (resembling parsley). It grows to a height of about 45 cm (18 in) and prefers a rich, moderately moist growing medium in a sunny position. We use the delicate aniseed-flavoured leaves in salads, sandwiches, and fish and egg dishes. Culpeper's Herbal says that it is good for bruises and swellings.

CHIVES
A hardy, low-growing, clump-forming perennial, with green, tubular stems topped with round, rose-pink flowerheads that likes a rich, well-watered medium in a sheltered, sunny corner. We use the distinctive onion-like stems and leaves in sandwiches and omelettes. Used traditionally by herbalists to stimulate the appetite and as a cold cure.

DILL

A hardy annual with tall stems topped with feathery, blue-green leaves that grows to a height of about 60–90 cm (2–3 ft) and likes a well-drained, moderately fertile medium in a sheltered, sunny position. We use the freshly picked leaves to garnish and flavour new potatoes and white fish. Culpeper's Herbal says that it is good for curing wind, easing pain and encouraging rest.

FENNEL

A hardy herbaceous perennial with tall stems, feathery, green leaves and golden flowerheads that grows to a height of 1.5–1.8 m (5–6 ft) and likes a moist, well-drained, moderately fertile growing medium in a sheltered, sunny position. We use the leaves with fish, salads, stews, cakes and bread. Culpeper's Herbal says that it is good as a rub for cramps and as a wash for tired eyes.

MINT

Common mint is a hardy herbaceous perennial with mid-green leaves that grows to a height of about 60 cm (2 ft) and likes a moisture-retentive, fertile growing medium in a warm, sheltered position. We use the leaves chopped with brown sugar and mixed with vinegar to make mint sauce. Used traditionally by herbalists for clearing the head, and as a rub to help with scurf and dandruff.

PARSLEY

A hardy biennial that tends to be grown as an annual, with curly, tightly packed green leaves. It likes a moisture-retentive, fertile growing medium in full sun or shade. We use the leaves in sauces and as a garnish. Culpeper's Herbal says that it is good for earache and as a wash for swollen eyes.

ROSEMARY

An evergreen shrub with narrow, spiky, mid- to dark green, aromatic leaves that grows just about anywhere. We use the leaves to flavour fish and meat dishes. We always have a bunch of rosemary hanging at the head of the bed.

SAGE

A hardy evergreen shrub with long, aromatic, green-grey leaves that likes a fertile growing medium in a warm, sheltered spot. We use the leaves to flavour sage-and-onion stuffing, cheese dips and nut roasts. Sage has long been used to help with sore throats. My granny used to chop the leaves and mix them with apple cider vinegar and honey to ease a sick headache and sore throat.

THYME

A hardy, dwarf, evergreen shrub with small, aromatic leaves that likes a light, well-drained growing medium in an airy, sunny position. We use the leaves with fish and rich meats like hare and pork. Traditionally, thyme has been used for curing just about everything from warts and swellings to wind and joint aches.

WARNING
If you intend to use unfamiliar herbs in a medicinal context (as a drink, drench, wash or rub), you must seek the advice of a qualified herbalist.

Soft fruit

BLACKBERRIES

We planted our blackberries in much the same way as raspberries, in a long bed with a good depth of fresh manure topped with well-rotted manure. We purchased the bare-rooted canes in late autumn and set them against a permanent, fence-like, post-and-wire support.

Troubleshooting

APHIDS Show as sticky curling leaves; spray in winter with a organic wash.

MOULD Show as a grey/white powder on leaves; remove and burn the leaves as and when they appear.

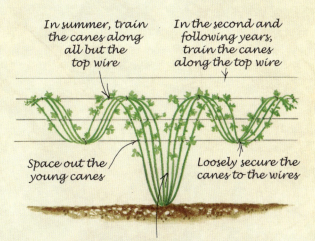

In summer, train the canes along all but the top wire

In the second and following years, train the canes along the top wire

Space out the young canes

Loosely secure the canes to the wires

After planting, cut the canes down to about 23 cm (9 in) above the ground

---

CURRANTS
(BLACK, RED AND WHITE)

Although the fruits look similar in shape and form, blackcurrants not only need to be treated slightly differently from red- and whitecurrants, but they are also generally easier to care for.

Troubleshooting

VANISHING BERRIES Birds will strip the berries if given a chance; avoid the problem by draping a netting tent over the bush.

DROOPING FOLIAGE Indicates lack of water; in dry weather, generously water when the sun goes down.

BLACKCURRANTS

First season after pruning

After planting, cut stems down to about 2.5 cm (1 in) above the ground; in the following season, cut out all shoots that have fruited

RED- AND WHITECURRANTS

Pruned as a bush

Cut main shoots back by half after planting; in late winter cut out shoots that cross the plant's centre

GOOSEBERRIES

In our experience, gooseberries do well against all the odds. One of our old neglected bushes, which must be at least 20 years old, gives us a surprising amount of golden fruits. We eat them served up in pies and crumbles and made into a delicious jam.

Troubleshooting

VANISHING BERRIES Birds will strip the berries if given a chance; avoid the problem by draping a netting tent over the bush.

APHIDS Show as sticky distorted leaves; spray or drench with an organic mix and remove and burn the debris from around the bush.

After planting, cut back each main branch by about half; in the following autumn, cut back all the shoots that formed in the year

At the end of the following season, shorten those shoots produced during the season by half and clear out any shoots that crowd the centre

RASPBERRIES

The raspberry is a hardy deciduous shrub, a member of the rose family. There are two kinds of raspberry: summer-fruiting and autumn-fruiting.

Troubleshooting

APHIDS Show as sticky curling leaves; spray with an organic wash, then a day or two later spray with water and remove and burn the debris.

VANISHING FRUIT Birds and squirrels may eat the fruit; drape the plants with a net.

Tie the new canes to the support wires; after fruiting, cut all fruiting canes down to ground level and tie up new canes

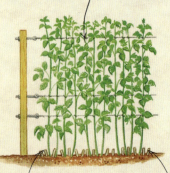

Summer-fruiting varieties – in spring, when the canes start to grow, cut the old dead wood down to ground level

Autumn-fruiting varieties – after fruiting, cut all the canes down to ground level

RHUBARB

Rhubarb is a vegetable that is generally treated as a fruit. Although it can be raised from seed, the swiftest and most common method of propagating is by root division. We enjoy rhubarb dished up hot with custard, cold with yogurt or ice cream, and used in a crumble or pie.

Troubleshooting

CROWN ROT Shows as a squidgy brown area; burn the plant, wash your tools and set a new resistant variety in a different bed.

Use a bucket to cover the dormant buds

Trim and compost both ends

Forced rhubarb

Protect with straw in winter

In late winter or early spring, divide the dormant roots, and set each piece in a 30 cm (1 ft) deep hole; fill the hole with garden compost and old manure

STRAWBERRIES

In a good year, our 20 or so strawberry plants give us a bowl every day throughout the picking season, as well as treats for friends and neighbours, and there is still enough to make into jam. Strawberries can be grouped into early, mid-season and late varieties; depending on the variety, plant in late summer, mid-autumn, early winter or spring.

Troubleshooting

VANISHING FRUIT Birds, squirrels, mice, slugs and kids are all pests; we drape the plants with a net, gather slugs as soon as they appear, set mice traps and encourage kids to help with picking.
DEBRIS Damp fallen leaves and fruit all encourage moulds and mildews; remove the debris, mulch with crisp, dry straw and generally keep the bed clean.

Plant 38 cm (15 in) apart with the crown above ground

Protect from birds as fruits form with nets

Spread the roots

Well-rotted manure

Mulch with straw

Peg down runner into pot to propagate

Tree fruits

Tree fruits, or top fruits, are fruits from trees that have been specifically grown for human food. Although worldwide there are many examples of tree fruits, everything from abiu, apple and almond to sweet chestnut, tamarillo and walnut, I have focused on the three common ones – apple, pear and plum – because they are relatively easy to source, they are straightforward to grow and they give good value for time and effort. Our orchard of a dozen or so apple trees, three plums and four pears gives us enough fruit for eating, giving to friends and family, freezing and jam making. Anything we don't consume gets eaten by the geese.

APPLES

There are hundreds of varieties and types to choose from: dessert apples that are held in the hand and crunched, apples that are cooked, trees as big as a house and trees that grow no higher than a human. A good tree will give you food for a lifetime. Go for varieties that you personally like, and then choose something like a bush on an M27 rootstock that grows to a height of about 1.8 m (6 ft) or perhaps a compact column on a MM106 rootstock that grows to about 2.4 m (8 ft). Plant a range of varieties so that you have a long picking period.

Bare-rooted trees must be planted between autumn and spring, while container-grown tress can be planted all year.

PRUNE In late autumn.
HARVEST In mid-summer to late autumn.
STORE We store first-class, hand-picked apples wrapped in newspaper and packed in boxes, mix some with plums to make jam, and boil the rest down and freeze.

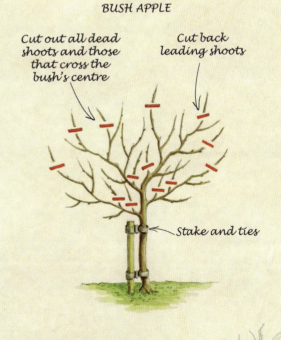

BUSH APPLE

Cut out all dead shoots and those that cross the bush's centre

Cut back leading shoots

Stake and ties

ESPALIER PEAR

When the top tier of wires is reached, cut off the leading shoot

Espaliers need a strong framework of posts and wires secured to a wall

Cut back the ends of the arms, as suggested

PEARS

There are hundreds of varieties to choose from: dessert pears as soft and juicy as plums, pears so hard they must be cooked, trees that yield 45–110 kg (100–250 lb) of fruit, and trees that are best grown against a wall. A good tree will feed you and your family. Best advice in the first instance is to go for varieties that you personally like. We have eight trees of two varieties: Conference that gives a good-sized pear with a firm, crisp bite, and an old William type that gives a huge fat fruit perfect for cooking.

Bare-rooted trees must be planted between autumn and spring, while container-grown trees can be planted all year.

PRUNE In late autumn to early winter.
HARVEST In mid-summer to late autumn.
STORE We eat the choice ones fresh and cook the rest.

BUSH PLUM

Cut back new shoots

Ensure that the trunk is secured to a stake

PLUMS

Plums are easy to grow and generally good croppers. As with apples and pears, go for a variety that you know and like, or a dwarfing variety that matures at a height of about 2.7–5 m (9–16 ft).

Bare-rooted trees must be planted between mid- and late autumn, while container-grown trees can be planted all year.

PRUNE In early spring for training, and early to mid-summer for an established tree. Note that some varieties need a lot of pruning.
HARVEST In mid-summer to late autumn.
STORE We eat some fresh, mix some with apples to make jam, and freeze the rest as pulp.

Tractors

I was the sort of boy who loved playing with toy cars and construction kits, so it was not surprising that when we moved to Sun Valley Cottage the first thing I did was start to search out an old tractor. We now have a 1950s Ferguson diesel tractor complete with a range of implements and a heap of chains and ropes. We mow the meadow, cut the nettles, move logs from the woods through to the shed, lift and drag fallen trees, transport the beehives from one end of the garden to the other, and do all the things that we could not do with muscle power alone. It is easy to operate and maintain, it is cheap to run, and altogether good fun!

TRACTOR AND TRANSPORT BOX

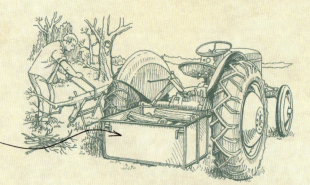

Transport box for moving heavy materials like firewood

TRAILER

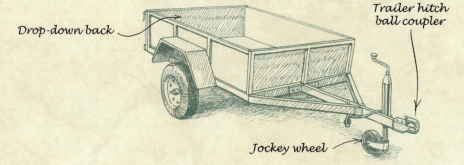

Trailer hitch ball coupler

Drop-down back

Jockey wheel

Implements

Implements are all the bits and pieces that go with the tractor – transport box, plough, trailer, mower, hedge cutter, trench digger and front loader. If you are a beginner, start with, say, a standard lift box – a large box that fits on the lifting mechanism, used to lift things like logs and churns – and then acquire other items when you have a clear understanding of your needs. Implements can easily be obtained second-hand from farm sales.

BUYING A TRACTOR

- If you want to get an old tractor, the best starting point is to visit a farming show where you can see lots of tractors and speak to enthusiasts.
- Our Ferguson tractor is beautiful – all the bearings are firm, it has never been repainted, and although it leaks a little oil the general condition suggests that it has been cared for.
- At the time of writing, a good second-hand Ferguson tractor can be bought for about a quarter of the price of a new Chinese mini-tractor.
- Tractors of this era are designed to run variously on petrol, a mix of petrol and oil, and diesel. Everyone tells us that diesel is the best option.
- When you go to see a second-hand tractor, try to start it from cold.
- Once you have the tractor running, drive it in a figure-of-eight pattern and check out the steering column bearings.
- Make sure that the huge castings that make up the body of the tractor are free from cracks.
- Nuts and bolts in good condition indicate that the tractor has been carefully maintained, while beaten-about nuts and bolts suggest that the machine has been abused.
- Look at the lifting mechanism and make sure it operates smoothly.

Animal husbandry

Keeping chickens
Chickens and self-sufficiency are a near perfect twosome. Chickens are easy to house, and they will recycle your kitchen and garden scraps, eat garden pests and weeds, give you unlimited amounts of high-nitrogen manure and, best of all, lay fresh eggs for most of the year.

Housing
Our chicken shed is a large walk-in type with full head height, a door wide enough for a wheelbarrow, an opening window, air vents and a range of nesting boxes that can be opened from outside. It allows us to collect the eggs and clean the shed out without getting backache, and the chickens to lead a comfortable life. The shed must be ringed with a chicken wire fence and a gate.

Feeding
Although we used to prepare our own feed mashes and formulas, we now feed our hens a mix of scraps from the kitchen and vegetable garden, corn from a local farmer, and top-quality layers' pellets; also, when the conditions are right, we let them loose from their enclosure to seek out their own food.

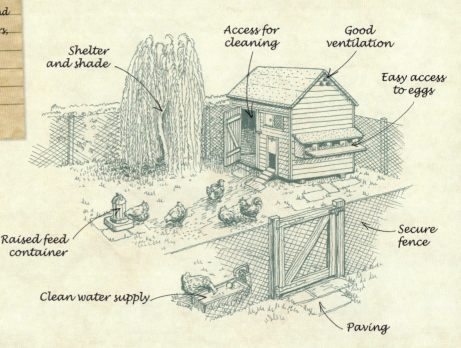

CHICKEN HOUSE AND RUN

Shelter and shade

Access for cleaning

Good ventilation

Easy access to eggs

Raised feed container

Clean water supply

Secure fence

Paving

Keeping geese
Geese need lots of space and grass. We have a total of 15 geese – three males and 12 females. There are two Chinese, a Toulouse, a Roman, six Embden and the rest are mixed. They give us eggs from late winter through to late spring – say a total of 600. This egg count might seem low, but remember that a goose egg is about three times the size of a hen's egg, and each goose egg sells at the same price as six hen's eggs.

Housing
Although we have a large goose house with a lean-to building on the side, our geese spend most of the time in the orchard. We use the shed for keeping the feed and for housing sick birds, while the geese use the lean-to for shade in summer, for shelter in windy weather and for laying. The main thing that we have learnt about geese is that each one is uniquely unpredictable.

Feeding
We let our geese have the run of the meadows and the woods, and only put them in at night. They eat grass, weeds and scraps from the kitchen and the vegetable garden in the spring and summer, and scraps, corn, cooked potatoes and porridge in the autumn and winter.

GEESE LEAN-TO

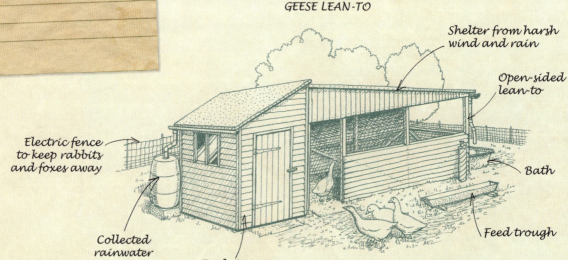

Shelter from harsh wind and rain

Open-sided lean-to

Electric fence to keep rabbits and foxes away

Bath

Collected rainwater

Feed trough

Feed storage

Keeping turkeys

While you might keep ducks, chickens and geese just for their eggs, the only real reason for keeping turkeys is for their meat. If you know about fattening ducks, chickens and geese, the good news is that turkeys are easier and less expensive. An easy-start option for beginners is to buy off-heat poults at about 6–8 weeks old.

Housing

The ideal for, say, ten turkeys is a pole barn type shelter, about 3 × 1.8 m (10 × 6 ft). It needs three closed sides, wire mesh and a gate on the fourth side, a dry floor made of something like wood, concrete or woodchip bedding, a round-cornered 7.5 cm (3 in) square perching pole fixed about 45 cm (18 in) off the floor, and a secure lean-to shed, for the feed and bedding, set to one side. The whole shelter should be enclosed in a chicken-wire run.

Feeding

We fed our last lot of off-heat turkeys a mix of potatoes, apples, bread, grass, greens from the garden, grain, pellets and just about anything else that was going. They did very well on it.

TURKEY HOUSE AND RUN

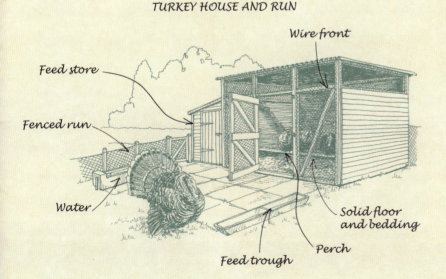

Wire front

Feed store

Fenced run

Water

Feed trough

Perch

Solid floor and bedding

BREEDS
There is a lot of interest in heritage breeds such as Bourbon Red, Standard Bronze and Narragansett. If you have a local heritage breeder who is producing other breeds, then go for them.

- Bourbon Red – brownish-red feathers, males weigh 15 kg (33 lb), females 8 kg (18 lb).
- Standard Bronze – blue-black iridescent feathers, males weigh 13 kg (29 lb), females 9.5 kg (21 lb).
- Narragansett – black-white feathers, males weigh 10.5 kg (23 lb), females 6.5 kg (14 lb).

Keeping sheep

We first got involved with sheep because Gill as a weaver wanted to spin her own wool, and I wanted to know everything from buying them at the market through to mating, breeding, lambing and shearing. The old adage is true: 'The best way of learning is by doing.'

Do you have enough ground for sheep?

Although much depends upon your set-up, you could run 3–4 ewes to 0.4 hectare (1 acre). This allows for each ewe to have two lambs – say three ewes and six lambs. You would need to split the plot with a fence so that you can rotate and rest the ground, and buy in winter feed. This system only works if you use a neighbour's ram and eat/sell the lambs in the autumn.

Thinking it through

Why do you want sheep? Do you simply want the experience, or the wool, or the meat? Sheep are a big commitment. You must be on hand to feed and water, inspect the fencing, check for parasites and diseases, watch out for dogs, and oversee the lambing. If you plan to have lambs, are you prepared for the emotional jolt of eating them or parting with them?

LAMBING AND SHEARING SHED

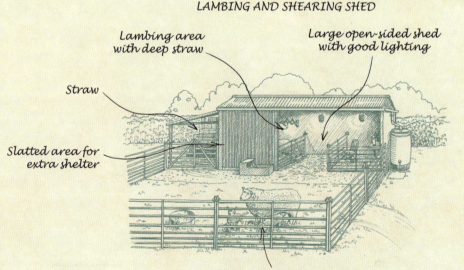

Lambing area with deep straw

Large open-sided shed with good lighting

Straw

Slatted area for extra shelter

Interlocking hurdles can be reconfigured to suit location

Breeding facts – things you need to know

· Sheep are sexually mature in their second year.

· Ewes mated in autumn will produce lambs about 21 weeks later in the following spring.

· When a ewe is ready to lamb, she will look ill at ease and eventually lie down and start groaning and straining.

· The birthing sequence is as follows: the ewe settles down in a shelter or in the lea of a wall or hedge, then the water bag appears, followed by the lamb's nose and two feet, and finally the head and shoulders. If you are a novice, you will need experienced help.

· Once the lamb is out, the mother will start licking the mess away from the lamb's face.

· Newborn lambs must be kept reasonably dry and out of cold winds. You risk losing a newborn lamb if you allow it to get wet and cold.

· The lambs must suckle within a couple of hours of being born.

· Orphan lambs can be bottle-fed with formula milk, just like a baby. Be mindful if you take on feeding that the lamb will need to be fed regularly – say four times during a 24-hour period.

WARNING Some sheep diseases can cross over to humans – especially to pregnant women and young children – so talk to your vet.

Housing

Apart from a rough shelter at lambing time, sheep live most of their lives out of doors. A swift, low-cost option is to build a temporary shelter from bales of straw, corrugated iron, poles and rope.

Shelters

You will need a simple, three-sided, barn-type shelter complete with hurdles and gates where you can store the feed and carry out the various husbandry procedures, such as trimming feet, feeding lambs and shearing (see opposite).

Feeding facts

• Sheep can thrive on average to poor pasture.
• Before and after lambing, the ewes will need extra food – corn, chopped swedes, or concentrated pellets.
• To fatten lambs, feed swedes, hay and linseed cake.
• In winter, feed ewes with hay, plus a rising intake of supplements.

Shearing

When we got our first sheep, we visited an ancient farmer who showed us how to shear a sheep with a pair of hand clippers. He up-ended and straddled the animal – so that he was holding the sheep under the chin and looking down at the belly – and then he simply cut and eased the wool away from the body. He also showed us how, in high summer when the weather is blazing hot, it is possible to pluck and roll the fleece away from the sheep. We later learnt that this system is known in Shetland as 'rooing'.

Sheep for eating

When the time comes for slaughter, make contact with your vet and a registered abattoir and let them guide you through the procedures.

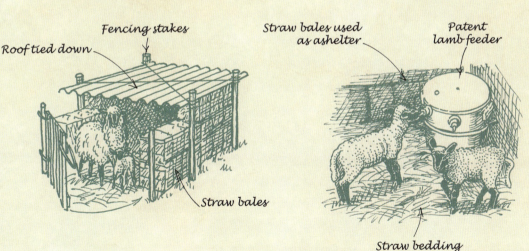

A TEMPORARY SHELTER

Roof tied down
Fencing stakes
Straw bales

FEEDING ORPHANED LAMBS

Straw bales used as ashelter
Patent lamb feeder
Straw bedding

Keeping llamas and alpacas

Llamas and alpacas come from South America, where llamas were bred as beasts of burden and alpacas for their fleeces. At 45–68 kg (100–150 lb) an adult alpaca weighs about half as much as a llama.

The rule of thumb is 3–5 llamas or 5–10 alpacas to 0.4 hectare (1 acre). If your land is already fenced for sheep – with say 1.2 m (4 ft) wire-netting topped with barbed wire – remove the barbed wire and replace it with another 30 cm (1 ft) or so of fencing. Llamas and alpacas only provide two sources of income – fibre and live sales.

WARNING At about two years of age, male llamas grow long, fang-like, fighting teeth and are given to butting.

Breeds
Make contact with a registered breeder and see what is on offer in your area.

Breeding facts
• Female llamas produce one offspring per year, called a cria (pronounced 'creeeah').

• The gestation period is about 350 days for a llama and 335 days for an alpaca.

• They give birth standing, usually in the daytime.

• Send for a vet if a birthing llama or alpaca falls over.

Housing
Llamas and alpacas can be housed like a pony in a three-sided field shelter. They need shade, shelter from cold winds and a good source of water.

Feeding facts
• Llamas and alpacas eat grass, foliage and just about anything that is going.
• A bale of hay will feed an adult llama for a week.
• In winter they need a supplementary feed such as corn and rolled oats.

Shearing
Llamas and alpacas are sheared in much the same way as sheep (see page 121).

LLAMA/ALPACA
FIELD SHELTER

Open front

Water butt

Keeping goats

We first kept goats because we wanted the milk for our wheezy baby and we had a liking for goat's cheese. Decide on your needs – milk, cheese, breeding, spinning and/or eating – and then get your goats from a recommended specialist.

HOUSING

Two goats need a shed about 2.4 m (8 ft) square, so each goat has a stall about 2.4 m (8 ft) long and 1.2 m (4 ft) wide. There must be water, plenty of cupboard space and a milking area to one side. The compound needs a 1.2–1.5 m (4–5 ft) high wire-mesh fence.

FEEDING

GOATS INDOORS need water, hay, salt lick and daily feed of oats/maize/ concentrate

GOATS OUTDOORS need scrubland for browsing plus 5.5 kg (12 lb) of hay a day in cold weather

GOATS IN MILK must have a supplement of oats/hay/special feed

Breeding facts

- The female is ready for mating at 18 months old.

- She will be ready in the autumn, when the vulva shows wet and red and the tail wags.

- She will have a three-day long season every 21 days.

GOAT HOUSING

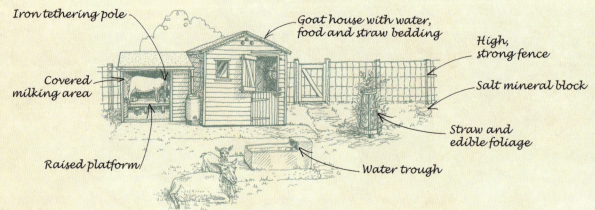

Iron tethering pole

Goat house with water, food and straw bedding

High, strong fence

Covered milking area

Salt mineral block

Straw and edible foliage

Raised platform

Water trough

• The easiest option for mating is to take your goat to stud.

• The gestation period is about 150 days.

• When she is due, her udder will start to fill, the vulva will show a discharge and she will become unsettled.

• You will need experienced help for the first birth.

Milking

Leave the mother with the kid(s) for about two weeks and then start milking once or twice a day. To do this, put the goat on a leash, stand her on a platform so that she is at a comfortable working height, clip the leash to the wall, fit a hobble on her back legs, and wash the udder with warm water. Encircle a single teat with thumb and fingers, gently squeeze with the thumb so that the milk is contained and apply a gentle downward stroking movement. Waste the first squirt and then direct the milk into your pail.

- Jersey - medium-sized, light brown coat, good house cow, medium-yield rich-cream milk, needs housing in winter.
- Dexter - small, black or red coat, good to milk, high yielding.
- Friesian - large, black and white coat, very high milk yield.

Keeping a cow
Although keeping a cow is good fun, rewarding and a pleasure — as much milk, butter, cheese and animal companionship as you can take — it is without doubt a year-round commitment.

Things you need to know
- During winter, one cow will eat about a tonne of hay.

- If you buy in the hay, you need a minimum of 0.4 hectares (1 acre).

- You have to milk every day — twice for maximum yield or once for low yield.

BREEDING FACTS
- Cows are ready to be put to the bull or artificially inseminated when they are about two years old.

- A cow can only be mated when she is in heat, usually indicated by a mucus discharge and skittish behaviour.

- The gestation period is about nine months.

- It is traditional to have your cow mated in summer so she calves in spring.

- When the cow's time is near, her udders fill and her back end goes slack.

- The birthing order is as follows: the water bag appears, followed closely by a nose and two feet, and then the head and shoulders.

- Once out, the mother will lick the calf into action.

- You will need experienced help on hand for the birth.

Housing
The ideal is a shelter big enough for storing the hay and for milking.

Milking
Encircle the teat with thumb and fingers and gently squeeze down with a rolling action. Cows are happiest when there is plenty of food, warm hands and a feeling of calm.

Weaning options

• Let the calf have all the milk for a week and then gradually take it away to feed from a bucket.

• Milk the cow and give half to the calf.

• You and the calf can have two teats each for the first month.

• Let the calf feed for a limited number of hours per day.

COW SHED AND MILKING AREA

Water butt

Water trough

Concrete floor
(front of shed removed for clarity)

Keeping pigs

Keeping pigs The only reason to keep pigs is for their meat. It is best to start with a couple of weaners and then, maybe, get involved in other options when you have a clearer understanding of your aims, skills and needs. A weaner is a pig that is strong and healthy enough to be removed from the sow, which occurs at 6–9 weeks, depending upon breed and general health.

Things you need to know

- Pigs are social animals – they enjoy company. A pair of happy pigs will fatten up faster than a single, lonely pig, or pigs that are in any way distressed.

- Pigs are happiest when they are living outdoors, rooting about in the soil, digging wallows, getting muddy and generally being a pig.

- You will need to set up a post-and-wire stock fence and reinforce it with a modern electric fence just inside the boundary.

- Although pigs will eat just about everything, and while they have traditionally been fed on swill from restaurants, you must restrict the waste to things like bread, fruit pies, fruit and vegetables, chips, buns – no bits of chicken or meat pies.

- Pigs can only be moved with an animal movement licence – make contact with your local animal health and safety department.

CHOOSING A BREED

A good option in the context of self-sufficiency is to go for one of the older rare breeds - they are hardier, tougher and better able to take care of themselves.

- Large Black --Large, black-haired, traditional lop-eared, docile, good-natured, ideal for keeping outdoors.
- Tamworth - Good size, sandy or reddish colour, long snout, good for keeping outdoors.
- Saddleback - There are two saddleback breeds, Essex Saddleback and Wessex Saddleback, both are black and white banded, hardy, very good for keeping outdoors.
- Gloucester Old Spot - One of the less common breeds, can be white with black spots or vice versa, hardy, docile, generally good-natured, good for outdoors.

MOVABLE ARK FOR PIGS

Ark provides shelter from sun, wind and rain

Trees for shade

Electric fence can easily be relocated

Mud wallow

Boards contain bedding and young piglets

Secured water trough

Housing

A pig house can be just about anything from a specially built sty made from brick and tiles through to a temporary shelter made from hay bales topped with sheets of corrugated iron. Anything will do as long as it is strong, low to the ground and built so that it will keep off the sun, wind and rain.

Feeding facts

· Pigs thrive on routine. They must be fed at regular intervals 2–3 times a day.

· Traditionally, a pig was given as much food as it could eat in 20 minutes.

· Pigs must have water on demand.

· Weaners need three good feeds a day, plus all they can find.

· Pigs on grass need supplementary feeds – low feed with good grass, good feed with poor grass.

· Feed basic meals for the first 16 weeks and then feed to fatten.

· Pigs thrive on wild food – acorns, sweet chestnuts, beechnuts, elderberries.

Keeping bees

Having bought an 'overwintered colony' from specialists, we loaded our bee suits, travel lids and luggage straps in the car and went. When we arrived, we admitted that we were complete beginners. They explained everything: how we should put on our suits, how we should handle the bees, how when we got home we should transfer the bees to the main hive, and so on. They were true mentors.

The working year

Note that the precise timing will vary according to your location.

- LATE SUMMER Most of the honey will have been extracted. Feed the bees with syrup in readiness for winter.

- EARLY AUTUMN Consider re-queening if the existing queen is more than two years old. Remove supers. Continue feeding until the hive is full of winter stores.

- MID-AUTUMN Reduce the size of the entrance and fit a mice guard. Make sure there is plenty of ventilation. Fit a windbreak and hive straps.

- LATE AUTUMN Remove weeds and debris from the hives.

- EARLY WINTER Relax and enjoy the honey.

- MID-WINTER Check that the hives are secure.

- LATE WINTER Have a look in the hive if the temperature rises to 10°C (50°F) or more. If the stores are low, give the bees an emergency feed of candy.

- EARLY SPRING If the stores look low, give syrup in top feeders, plus pollen patties.

- MID-SPRING Bees will be fully operational. They will be expanding in numbers, so add supers as necessary.

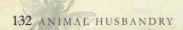

DRONE

QUEEN

WORKER

• LATE SPRING The hive is expanding, so add more supers and have an empty hive on hand for a possible captured swarm.

• EARLY SUMMER Make sure there is plenty of water. Monitor the number of mites.

• MID-SUMMER Start extracting honey.

• LATE SUMMER Put extracted supers and honey-extracting equipment well away from the hives so that they can be cleaned up by the bees. Put the extracted supers in the freezer to kill moths.

NATIONAL HIVE

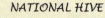

Metal-covered roof

Ventilation slot

Crown board

Super with 11 frames

Queen excluder

11 brood frames - bees build comb on the reinforced wax sheets

Brood chamber

Varroa open-mesh floor

Entrance block

TOOLS

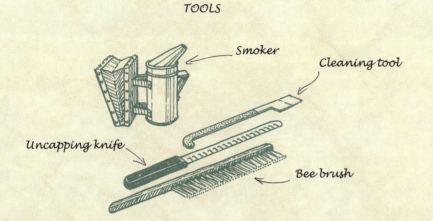

Smoker

Cleaning tool

Uncapping knife

Bee brush

Fitting the supers

A honey super (a shallow box containing 8–10 slender wooden frames that in turn support sheets of beeswax foundation) is the part of the beehive that is used to collect honey. The act of putting a super on top of the brood box with the express intention of collecting honey is termed 'supering'.

Adding the first super

Fit the first super when the brood chamber is fully occupied and bursting with bees, and the bees have started work on the outer faces of the two outer frames – it is much better to be early than a bit late. Having donned your bee suit, light the smoker, and place the super, complete with the frames of foundation, a queen excluder and the hive tool, comfortably to hand. Puff smoke around the entrance of the hive, wait a minute, remove the roof and the crown board and search each of the frames for the queen and queen cells. When you find the queen, make sure she is out of harm's way. If and when you find the queen cells, either partially or completely formed, destroy them with the hive tool, and note that you will have to make another check in seven days' time. When the job is done, place the queen excluder on top of the brood chamber so that the wires/slots are running counterwise with the brood frames, set the super complete with its frames of foundation on top of the queen excluder, and replace the crown board and the roof.

EXTRACTING AND BOTTLING HONEY

1 Take the supers and set them in the extractor so that they all face in the same direction.

2 Turn the handle and spin the honey into the outer bin. Repeat this procedure with all the supers.

3 When the extractor is full, pour the honey through a sieve and into a large plastic bin.

4 Put all the used sticky items out in the garden for the bees to clean.

5 Leave the honey in the bin until it has settled, and then pour it into small plastic tubs.

6 Pour the honey into 0.4 kg (1 lb) jars as needed.

7 Write the date on the jar and, if it is to be sold, prepare and label according to government body regulations.

Glossary

· APIARY A group of hives; the ideal is a sheltered, sunny area well away from overhanging trees and public footpaths.

· BASE The base on which the hive sits; this might be anything from a wooden frame with legs to a stack of concrete blocks.

· BEE SPACE A 6–9 mm (¼–⅜ in) space between component parts of the hive.

· BEE SUIT A protective outfit with a hat, veil and gloves.

· BOTTOM BOARD The solid wood or wire-mesh floor of a beehive.

· BROOD CHAMBER The part of the hive in which the brood is reared.

· COMB FOUNDATION Sheets of beeswax, stamped with a cell pattern.

· FEEDING The procedure of giving the bees a feed of sugar or syrup.

· FRAME A slender wooden structure designed to hold a honeycomb.

· HIVE The total structure, either a traditional, double-walled, picture-book or a simple box type; some modern hives are made of plastic and polystyrene.

· PESTS AND ENEMIES Bees are attacked by mice, ants, birds, wasps and all manner of mites, moulds and bugs.

· QUEEN EXCLUDER A mesh-like device made from wood, metal or plastic that limits the queen's movement around the hive.

· SMOKER Used to puff smoke which relaxes the bees.

· SUPERS Any part of the hive used for storing honey.

INSPECTING THE HIVE

All-in-one suit with built-in veil

Cowhide gauntlet gloves

Brood frame

National hive

Entrance

Keeping rabbits

Keeping rabbits If you eat meat, there is every reason why rabbits should figure highly in your self-sufficient scheme – they are tasty and have almost no fat. Two well-tended females and a single male will give you 50 offspring a year.

Housing

A good set-up for two females is a hut, about 90 cm (3 ft) square, with a linked wire pen that is about 2.4 m (8 ft) long, 1.2 m (4 ft) wide and 90 cm (3 ft) high; you will also need extra huts and runs for expansion. These sizes are well over the minimum recommended standards.

Feeding

Rabbits will eat just about everything from grasses, wild strawberries, dandelions and plantains to peas, carrots, herbs, greens, bark, twigs and buds. Give your caged rabbits a broad mix of foraged food – greens gathered from the hedgerows, woods and field margins – plus kitchen waste and a supplement of rabbit pellets.

Breeding facts – things you need to know

· They can be mated when they are 5–6 months old.

· For mating, always take the female to the male.

· The mating should occur almost immediately – if the female runs away, try again another day.

· After a mating, put the female back in her cage and repeat the procedure later the same day.

· The female is an induced ovulator, meaning she will only produce eggs after stimulation.

· The gestation period is about 31 days.

· A few days prior to birthing, put the female in a little nest box of her own.

· The young can be weaned at about 4–8 weeks.

BREEDS

· Californian – litter size 6-8, ready at 8-12 weeks, meat weight 3.5-5.5 kg (8-12 lb).

· New Zealand – litter size 8-10, ready at 8-12 weeks, meat weight 4-4.5 kg (9-10 lb).

· Champagne d'Argent – litter size 4-5, ready at 10-12 weeks, meat weight 4.5-7 kg (10-15 lb).

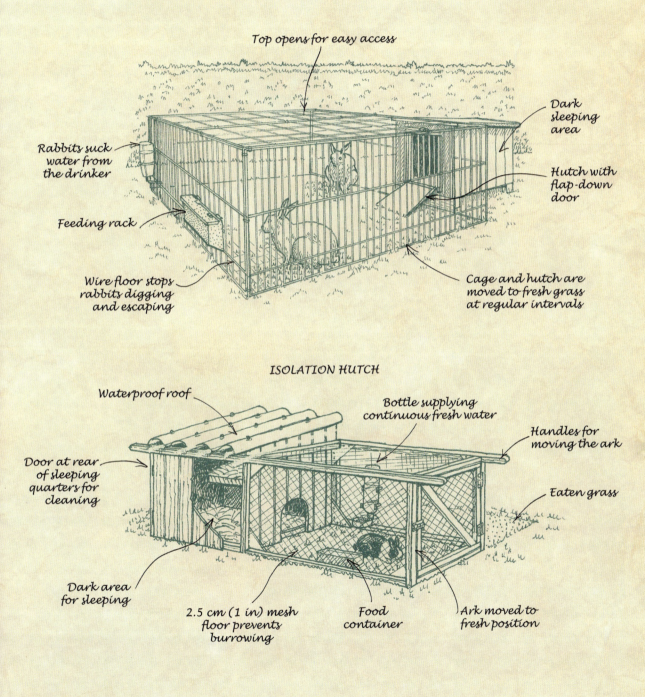

RABBIT HUTCH

Top opens for easy access

Dark sleeping area

Rabbits suck water from the drinker

Hutch with flap-down door

Feeding rack

Wire floor stops rabbits digging and escaping

Cage and hutch are moved to fresh grass at regular intervals

ISOLATION HUTCH

Waterproof roof

Bottle supplying continuous fresh water

Handles for moving the ark

Door at rear of sleeping quarters for cleaning

Eaten grass

Dark area for sleeping

2.5 cm (1 in) mesh floor prevents burrowing

Food container

Ark moved to fresh position

Homemaking

Making hard Caerphilly cheese

Caerphilly cheese originates in the villages around Caerphilly in south Wales. It is a good hard cheese, it is easy to make, it slightly 'grumbles' and it is ready to eat in about three weeks.

You need
- Double saucepan large enough to hold 4.5 litres (1 gallon)
- Cooking thermometer
- Large sieve
- Muslin
- Cheese press, or a tub and weight
- All the usual kitchen equipment

Ingredients
- 4.5 litres (1 gallon) milk
- 60 g (2 oz) starter powder
- ¼ teaspoon liquid rennet
- 1 tablespoon salt

Method

1 Heat the milk up to 32°C (90°F), stir in the starter powder and let it sit for about 30 minutes.

2 Mix the rennet with a little water and stir it into the milk, then let it sit at 32°C (90°F) for 50–60 minutes.

3 When the milk has turned into a thick rubbery curd, take a long knife and slice it into small cubes.

4 Drain the cubes through the sieve, empty the cubes into the saucepan, mix in the salt and tip the contents into the muslin-lined cheese press or tub.

5 After 30 minutes or so, unwrap the cheese and put in on a rack to air-dry.

6 Wrap it in greaseproof paper and put it in the fridge.

7 Inspect it every day; if you see mould, wipe it over with a vinegar-soaked cloth and change the greaseproof paper. Eat when the cheese is about three weeks old.

CHEESE-MAKING
EQUIPMENT

Double
saucepan

Cheese
press

Muslin

Sieve

Making butter

If you have more milk than you can drink, or you can buy surplus full-cream milk from a neighbouring farmer, then you should schedule making butter into your self-sufficient scheme.

You need
- Piece of cotton muslin about 90 cm (3 ft) square
- Large, low plastic bowl or pan
- Large flat skimming spoon
- Large stainless steel pan
- Dairy thermometer
- Large food mixer or butter churn
- Wooden board
- Pair of butter paddles
- Greaseproof paper

Ingredients
As much full-cream milk as you can manage

Method
1 Strain the milk through the muslin into the bowl, and leave to cool.

2 Twice next day, about eight hours apart, use the spoon to skim off the cream. Put the cream in the pantry, and after the second skimming give the skimmed milk to the livestock.

3 About 30 hours later, when the cream is slightly sour, put the cream into the pan, heat it up and hold it at 63°C (145°F) for 30 seconds.

4 Remove the cream from the heat and put it in the pantry.

5 Next day, when the cream is at room temperature, put it into the mixer or butter churn and set it to a slow, easy motion.

6 Continue until you have a large blob of butter (give the buttermilk to the family).

7 Chill the butter, put it on the wooden board and shape it with the paddles.

8 Finally wrap the butter in greaseproof paper and store it in the pantry.

BUTTER-MAKING EQUIPMENT

Food mixer

Double saucepan

Muslin

Thermometer

Skimming spoon

Paddles

Making farmhouse brown bread rolls

Real homemade bread rolls are swift and easy to make, and wonderfully satisfying. Biting into a warm, buttered, homemade brown bread roll is an experience that should not be missed.

You need
- Two baking trays
- All the usual kitchen equipment

Ingredients
- 10 teaspoons dried yeast
- 1.2 litres (2½ pints) water
- 3 teaspoons treacle
- 1.4 kg (3 lb) strong brown flour
- 3 teaspoons virgin olive oil
- 6 teaspoons salt

Method

1 Grease the baking trays and warm them in a preheated oven at 120°C (250°F) for 10 minutes.

2 Sprinkle the yeast into 350 ml (¾ pint) warm water and leave for 5 minutes.

3 Stir the treacle into the mix, leave for 10 minutes and add the rest of the water.

4 Mix the flour, olive oil and salt in a large bowl, add the yeasty mix and stir in.

5 Use your hands to knead the dough to make a large, slightly sticky ball.

6 Divide the dough into rounded, egg-sized lumps, put them on the baking trays, cover with tea towels and leave for about 30 minutes.

7 Bake in a preheated oven at 220°C (425°F) for 30 minutes, then lower the temperature to 200°C (400°F) and bake for another 15 minutes.

8 Turn the rolls out onto a rack to cool.

BREAD-MAKING EQUIPMENT

Measuring scales

Mixing bowl

Baking trays

Measuring jug

Yeast

Spoons and knife

Salt

YOU NEED

- Press/juicer/liquidizer/ bucket and cudgel (anything that will turn apples into pulp)
- Two plastic buckets
- Two 23-litre (5-gallon) plastic fermentation buckets complete with lids

- Two pieces of cotton muslin big enough to cover the fermentation buckets
- Room thermometer
- Two 23-litre (5-gallon) plastic fermentation barrels complete with airlocks and taps
- 90 cm (3 ft) length of 6 mm (¼ in) diameter clear flexible plastic tube

Making farmhouse cider

The wonderful thing about farmhouse cider, and the reason why you should include it in your self-sufficiency adventure, is its simplicity. Its amazing, life-enhancing taste is a bonus. It could not be easier — just apples, muscle power, Mother Nature and time.

Gill and Alan's cider

Of all our storing and preserving activities, making cider is one of our favourites. We select a warm, sunny day at the end of the season when the grass in the orchard is carpeted with windfalls, then take our press, buckets, barrels, tables and a lunch of bread and cheese out to the orchard, set ourselves up under the trees and get to work. I rake up the apples and put them in buckets of water and Gill picks out anything that is rotten or suspect and gives it to the geese. That done, we put the apples into a large wooden bucket and use a couple of wooden cudgels to stomp them to a mushy pulp (you could use a kitchen blender). Next we put the pulp into the press and work away until the juice starts to flow.

We continue gathering, bashing mashing, pressing and straining until we have several plastic barrels of juice all nicely fitted with airlocks and taps. Halfway through the day we have a lunch of bread, cheese and apple juice, and the geese eat the pressed apple pulp.

Three months or so later, when the weather is icy and the hot summer days are long gone, we open the cider. If it is good, we drink it for pleasure, and if it tastes a bit vinegary we mix it with honey and use it for cooking and cough cures. Nothing gets wasted.

Ingredients

Windfall apples

Method

1 Gather your ripe, bruised windfall apples from a clean, grassy meadow orchard. Throw away anything that is rotten. Do not worry about bruises, wormholes and bloomy yeasty skins, as they are vital ingredients.

2 Crush/press/grind/beat the apples and collect the juice in the buckets.

3 Pour and sieve the juice into the fermentation buckets.

4 Cover the buckets with muslin, tie with string and loosely sit the lids in place.

5 Hold the juice at a comfortable living temperature – about 15–21°C (60–70°F).

6 Check several times a day to make sure it is nicely bubbling.

7 Once the brew has settled down and the bubbles have flattened out, siphon the cider into the barrels and fit the airlocks.

CIDER-MAKING EQUIPMENT

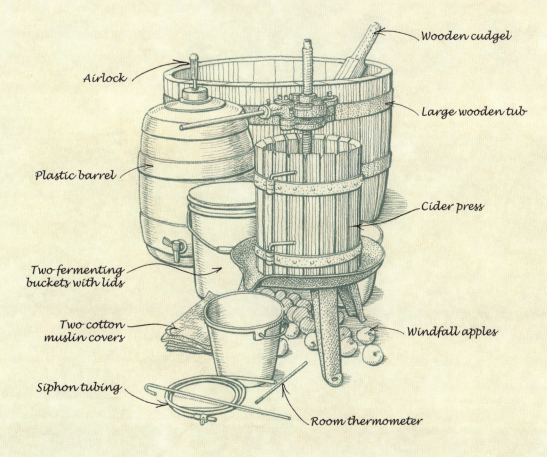

Wooden cudgel

Airlock

Large wooden tub

Plastic barrel

Cider press

Two fermenting buckets with lids

Windfall apples

Two cotton muslin covers

Siphon tubing

Room thermometer

FARMHOUSE APPLE AND DAMSON

A full-bodied country jam

Ingredients:

- 900 g (2 lb) damsons
- 900 g (2 lb) cooking apples
- 1.8 kg (4 lb) sugar
- 500 ml (1 pint) water

GILL'S APPLE AND BLACKBERRY

An easy-to-make favourite

Ingredients:

- 1.4 kg (3 lb) blackberries
- 450 g (1 lb) cooking apples
- 1.8 kg (4 lb) sugar
- 275 ml (½ pint) water

ALAN'S SEVILLE ORANGE MARMALADE

A lazy man's recipe

Ingredients:

- 900 g (2 lb) Seville oranges
- 2 large lemons
- 1.8 kg (4 lb) sugar
- 2.2 litres (4 pints) water

Making Gill's homely jam

For us, there are two types of jam: shop-bought stuff that looks good but tastes like a bad day at a chemical works, and our homely jam that looks a bit of a mess but tastes wonderful. In the context of jam-making, the term 'homely' is a Second World War term (quite complimentary) that means comfortable, honest and straightforward – less than exhibition quality.

General method

1 Take the fresh fruit and remove cores, pips, peel, stalks and any bad bits.

2 Smear the inside of the pan with a tiny knob of butter.

3 Weigh the fruit and slide it into the pan with the correct quantity of water.

4 Turn on the heat, bring to the boil and simmer until the fruit collapses.

5 Add the sugar, and simmer and stir for the appropriate time.

6 Test by spooning a dribble onto a very cold plate, waiting until it is cool and pushing with a fingernail – if it wrinkles, it is ready.

7 Turn off the heat, set the clean, dry, oven-sterilized jars on a wooden surface, and use a funnel and ladle to fill them up.

8 Set the waxed circles wax-side down on the surface of the hot jam and fit the covers.

9 Label and date, and store in a cool, dark cupboard.

JAM-MAKING EQUIPMENT

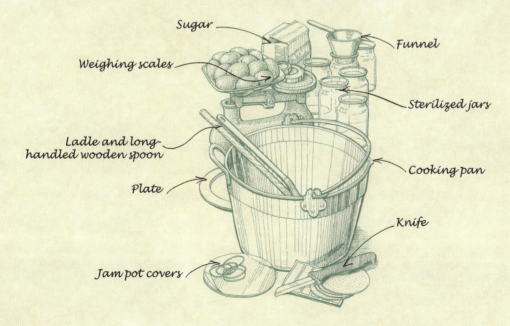

Sugar

Weighing scales

Ladle and long-
handled wooden spoon

Plate

Jam pot covers

Funnel

Sterilized jars

Cooking pan

Knife

Making chutney

Chutney making is a flexible way of using fruit and vegetables that would otherwise be difficult to save. For example, you have a glut of onions and cooking apples – some of them second-grade. You could pickle the onions and dry or bottle the apples, but chutney made from a mix of onions and apples is much easier and tastier, and it gives you a savoury option. Chutney is wonderful with fresh bread and homemade cheese.

GILL'S GREEN TOMATO CHUTNEY

A good way of using unripe tomatoes

Ingredients:

- 1.8 kg (4 lb) green tomatoes
- 450 g (1 lb) cooking apples
- 450 g (1 lb) onions
- 1 teaspoon salt
- 450 g (1 lb) brown sugar
- 500 ml (1 pint) vinegar
- 1 teaspoon each mustard, ginger and cayenne pepper

ALAN'S APPLE AND ONION SULTANA-FREE CHUTNEY

A good option if, like me, you have an aversion to sultanas

Ingredients:

- 1.8 kg (4 lb) cooking apples
- 900 g (2 lb) onions
- Handful of garlic cloves - to personal taste
- 1 teaspoon salt
- 1.4 kg (3 lb) brown sugar
- 1.7 litres (3 pints) vinegar
- 1 teaspoon each mustard, ground ginger and cayenne pepper

METHOD

1 Wash and prepare the ingredients, removing stalks, pips, cores and the like.

2 Chop finely or coarsely to taste.

3 Put the ingredients, bar the sugar, into the pan and cover with vinegar.

4 Turn on the heat and simmer for 1–4 hours until soft.

5 Pour the sugar into the mix, stir and simmer.

6 Put the washed jars in the oven and bring slowly up to heat.

7 Continue simmering and stirring until the mixture thickens.

8 Turn off the heat, set the jars on a board and use the ladle and funnel to fill the jars.

9 Fit the covers or lids and store in a cool, dark place.

BASIC CHUTNEY-MAKING EQUIPMENT

Weighing scales

Pickling vinegar

Stainless-steel pan

Jars and bottles

Cooking funnel

Chopping board

Mixing bowl

Jam-making labels

Knives

Bottling fruit and vegetables

Bottling is the process of preserving fruit and vegetables in thick-walled glass jars. Bottled fruit and vegetables have a unique taste and texture of their own. If you are aiming for off-grid self-sufficiency, bottling is a good, traditional, low-cost activity.

Homely method

1 Wash the jars and check there are new rubber seals/rings/lids to fit.

2 Select top-quality produce and prepare it according to its nature.

3 Pack the prepared produce in the jars.

4 Pour the prepared brine (30 g/1 oz cooking salt to 1.1 litre/2 pints boiling water) on top of the vegetables or the syrup (225 g/8 oz sugar to 550 ml/1 pint boiling water) on top of the fruit to cover.

5 Tap the jars to remove air bubbles and add more brine/syrup as necessary.

6 Wipe the rims and set the appropriate rubber rings/seals in place.

7 Sit the jars on a grid or trivet in a large saucepan or pan – with 2.5 cm (1 in) or so of water – on the heat. Slowly raise the temperature to boiling and simmer for 10–15 minutes at 85°C (185°F).

8 When the time is up, remove the lids, top the jars up with boiling water, swiftly clip or screw the lids in place and allow to cool.

9 Next day test the vacuum seal by removing the screw top/clip and lifting the jar up by its lid – have one hand held in readiness in case the seal fails.

Weighing scales

Sugar or salt

Jug

Cloths

Chopping board

Sterilized jars

Seals

Knife and spoon

Two large pans and wire grill (false base)

Thermometer

Freezing fruit and vegetables

If you can get fruit and vegetables for little or no cost (from garden gluts, foraged, or from local farmers' markets), you have exhausted your bottling, pickling and chutney- and jam-making capabilities, and you have low-cost electricity, there comes a time when freezing is arguably viable. Beans, peas and carrots are easy – we simply prepare them as for eating, blanch for 2 minutes, bag them up, cool in cold water and freeze. We cook apples to a stiff pulp with cloves and then freeze them. The excitement comes when we do what we call our 'special messes'.

How to make Alan and Gill's onion, aubergine, tomato and courgette mess

1 Prepare equal quantities of onions, courgettes, tomatoes and aubergines – all washed and chopped into large pieces.

2 Set a large wok/frying pan on the heat, dribble it with olive oil and swiftly fry the onions for about 30 seconds.

3 When the onions are soft, throw in equal quantities of the other three ingredients and gently stir and turn.

4 When the mix starts to sizzle, time it for 2 minutes – all the while turning – then bag it up in meal-size quantities and swiftly cool in cold water.

5 Repeat this until you and your supplies are exhausted, then freeze the lot.

6 This mess is perfect in stews, stir-fries and soups, as a pie/pancake filling and as a side vegetable.

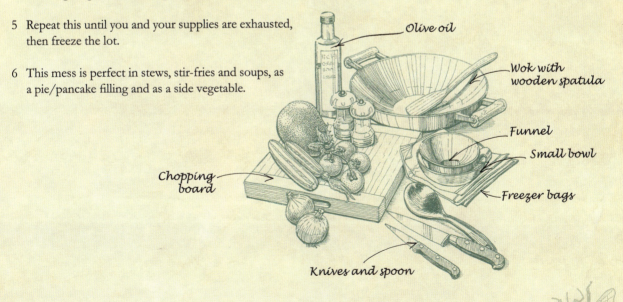

Olive oil

Wok with wooden spatula

Funnel

Small bowl

Freezer bags

Chopping board

Knives and spoon

Hand-sewing canvas and leather

When I was a kid, my self-reliant, ex-sailor grandfather showed me how to sew. His sort of sewing was all about using large curved and triangular-section needles and waxed cotton twine to work leather and canvas. He showed me four basic stitches – 'flat stitch', 'round stitch', 'baseball or handball stitch' and 'rope stitch' – and these have over the years enabled me to sew up sacks, make leather moccasins, sew on belt buckles, mend and make tarpaulins and tents, and so on.

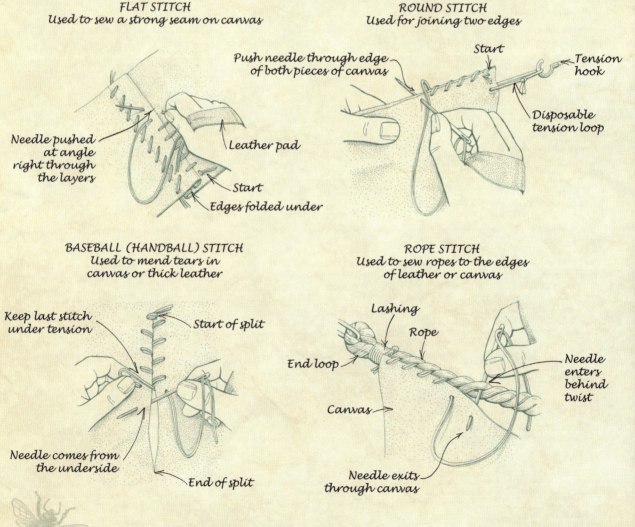

FLAT STITCH
Used to sew a strong seam on canvas

Push needle through edge of both pieces of canvas

Leather pad

Needle pushed at angle right through the layers

Start

Edges folded under

ROUND STITCH
Used for joining two edges

Start

Tension hook

Disposable tension loop

BASEBALL (HANDBALL) STITCH
Used to mend tears in canvas or thick leather

Keep last stitch under tension

Start of split

Needle comes from the underside

End of split

ROPE STITCH
Used to sew ropes to the edges of leather or canvas

Lashing

Rope

End loop

Canvas

Needle enters behind twist

Needle exits through canvas

Basic knitting

When my mum and gran unravelled old jumpers and washed, coiled and knitted the saved yarn into hats, gloves, socks and other things, we did not think of it as recycling – it was just a good, sensible, money-saving thing to do. If you want to save resources by make-do-and-mend, and/or use your spun wool, then knitting is perfect.

CASTING ON

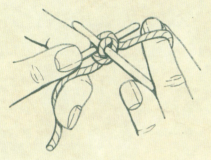

Make a loop on the left-hand needle and loosely knot to secure; pull a stitch on the left needle and slip on a new loop/stitch onto the same needle.

KNIT STITCH 1

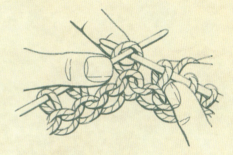

Insert the point of the right needle into the stitch on the left needle.

KNIT STITCH 2

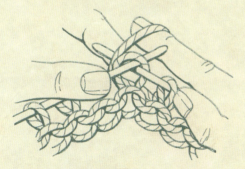

With your index finger, wind the yarn under and over the point of the right needle.

KNIT STITCH 3

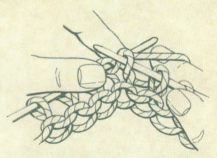

Using the right needle, pull a new stitch through the old stitch to form a loop, then slide the old stitch off the left needle.

Patchwork

Patchwork The great thing about patchwork, and the reason why it figures in self-sufficiency, is that it uses fabric that would otherwise be wasted. There are two types of patchwork: traditional geometrical patchwork – the quilts and cushions that our great-grannies made from little hexagonal scraps of fabric all put together with tiny, hand-sewn stitches – and rag patchwork made from torn strips of fabric, with the torn edges on view, all sewn on a machine.

HAND-SEWN HEXAGON PATCHWORK

Cover the hexagonal cardboard template with the fabric and tack it into place

One stitch for each fold

Sew the fabric-covered hexagons edge to edge

MACHINE-SEWN TORN-STRIP PATCHWORK

Mark out the backing fabric

Machine-sew the strips in place so that the ragged edges are on show

Pegged rag rugs

Pegged rag rugs, also known as tab rugs, peggy rugs, strip rugs, proddy rugs, hooky rugs and many other names, are simple fireside-type rugs or mats made from hessian – usually a sack – and strips of cloth cut from old clothes. When I was a kid, my Welsh granny always had a rag rug on the go. It was all very simple. My grandpa would cut the stitching from a hessian sack down one side and along the bottom, open it out, and pin it to a frame. We would all cut strips of rag from various old clothes and trim them to a point, and finally my granny would use a prodder made from an old fish-knife handle to push the ends of the rag down through the hessian.

Method

1 Cut rags into strips about 10 cm (4 in) long and 2.5 cm (1 in) wide, and trim the ends to a blunt point.

2 With the hessian stretched over a frame, poke a hole through the weave and push one end of a strip down through the hole.

3 Poke another hole about 6 mm (¼ in) away from the first and push the other end of the strip through.

4 Take another strip of rag, and poke one end through your second hole.

5 Poke a third hole about 6 mm (¼ in) away from your second hole and poke the other end through. Continue in this way.

6 At the end of the session, turn the sack over so you can see the 'right' side and tidy up by pulling all the ends to the same length.

7 When the rug is finished, take it from the frame and hem and over-sew around the edges.

Rug edge guide line
(work on back of rug)

Cut strips

Push one end
of the strip
through the
sacking

Poke the end of the
next strip through
the second hole

Strip ends on
right side of rug

Knots, nets and crochet

If you have ambitions to work towards self-sufficiency — building and making items in the home workshop and garden — there will be many times when you need to know how to tie an appropriate knot, make a simple net and do basic string crochet. For example, in one month I knotted a rope to make a halter, Gill used a crochet stitch and a heap of waste plastic to make a shopping bag and a doormat, and we both used a netting technique to rig up a support for the beans. Here are some examples.

CLOVE HITCH
for tying to rails and posts

FISHERMAN'S KNOT
for tying two ropes or lines together

SIMPLE NETS
Net made using simple double overhand - good for hammocks, feed bags and plant supports

NECK HALTER
for large domestic animals

CROCHET
Basic chain - can be made into anything (hats, bags, mats, blankets...)

Fingers maintain the tension of the yarn

Slip knot held between thumb and centre finger

Hook goes through the loop and under the yarn

Spinning

Spinning If you are interested in self-sufficiency and you have sheep – animals that have to be shorn – the logical follow-on is to spin the fleece into yarn. It is an amazingly therapeutic process that involves shearing and sorting the fleece, carding and rolling the individual fibres into 'rolags', and then using a spinning wheel to turn the rolags into the spun yarn.

1 SORTING THE FLEECE

Use your fingers to tease out the locks of wool, separating the fibres and removing the waste

2 CARDING

Arrange and hook the sorted locks onto one card

3 CARDING

The cards are stroked across the wool to achieve an even spread of fibres

4 ROLLING

Use the back of the cards to roll the fibres and create a 'rolag' of wool

5 SPINNING

The left hand controls the spin as it travels along the fibres of the rolag

As the spin advances, the fibres are drawn out and extended with the right hand

Lichen dyeing

Lichens are complex organisms that are both fungi and algae. There are tree lichens, marine lichens, rock lichens and others. If you go out into a moist wood or heathland and have a close look at old trees and large ancient rocks, those tight, low, grey-green, dry, moss-like, patchy growths that you see are likely to be lichens. Traditionally, they were used to dye fleece. If you have ambitions to dye your fleece or yarn delicate shades of yellow, brown, green, purple and grey, without the need for chemicals, lichens are a good option. It is a good idea to run trials and build up your own personal colour range.

Method

1 Go to the nearest wood, forest or moor and search the trees and rocks for various types of lichen. Group them according to type and carefully note their location.

2 Make a net bag from net curtains, old tights or whatever comes to hand, and stuff it full of one type of lichen.

3 Put the bag of lichen in a tub/boiler/large pan of water and bring it to the boil.

4 Put your fleece/skein of wool in the tub and simmer for 2–3 hours.

5 When the time is up, remove the wool, rinse in a plastic bowl until the water runs clear, and air-dry.

6 Save a sample and carefully note the type of lichen, the gather date, the amount of water and the overall procedures, so that you can replicate the colour another time.

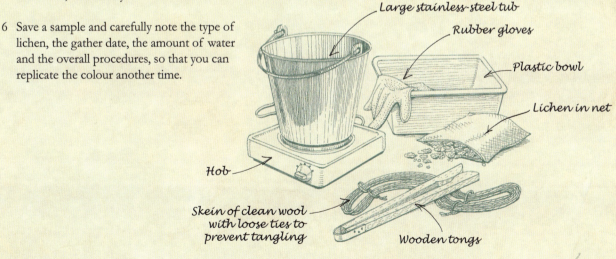

Large stainless-steel tub

Rubber gloves

Plastic bowl

Lichen in net

Hob

Skein of clean wool with loose ties to prevent tangling

Wooden tongs

Card weaving
Card weaving, sometimes called tablet weaving, is a ancient woven-textile technique used to create narrow bands, belts, trim and straps – things like harness, belts and decorative sashes. Square cards are threaded up – with a thread passing through each of the corner holes – and then the cards are selected and turned, either individually or in a pack, to create a 'shed' or space through which a weft thread is passed. The colour of the threads and the sequence of turning are the factors that shape the design. A good option for beginners is to thread up as shown, and to experiment with various turns.

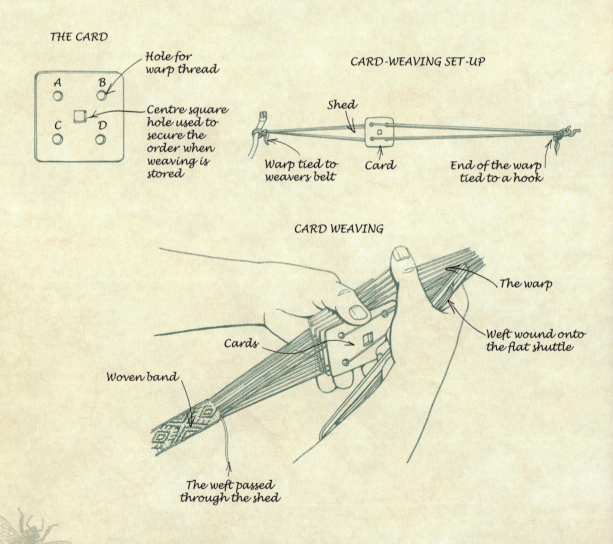

THE CARD

Hole for warp thread

A B
C D

Centre square hole used to secure the order when weaving is stored

CARD-WEAVING SET-UP

Shed

Warp tied to weavers belt

Card

End of the warp tied to a hook

CARD WEAVING

The warp

Weft wound onto the flat shuttle

Cards

Woven band

The weft passed through the shed

Making candles

Making beeswax candles is all pleasure: the dipping and rolling processes are wonderfully tactile, the wax smells good, and at the end the soft candlelight is a joy to the eye.

How to make dipped candles

1 Cut the tops off the bottles. Set one bottle aside, and put the other bottle in the pan and secure it with the wire.

2 Put water in the pan and in the set-aside bottle, and sliced up beeswax in the wired bottle.

3 Turn on the heat. When the wax has melted, take about 60 cm (2 ft) of string, hold it as shown, and dip the two ends into the wax and then out and into the water.

4 Straighten out the kinked wicks and repeat the dipping process until you have a pair of candles.

- Two plastic bottles
- Soft wire
- Pan large enough to take one bottle
- Enough beeswax to suit your needs
- Cotton candle wick – length to suit
- Kitchen items such as knives and scissors

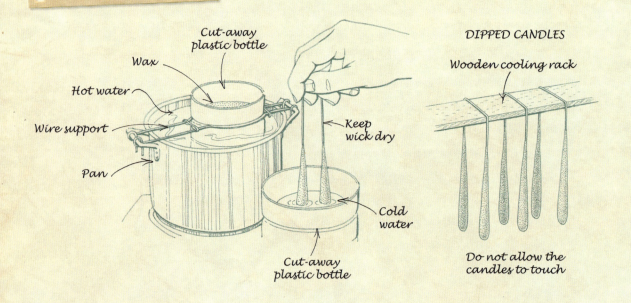

Cut-away plastic bottle

Wax

Hot water

Wire support

Pan

Keep wick dry

Cold water

Cut-away plastic bottle

DIPPED CANDLES

Wooden cooling rack

Do not allow the candles to touch

How to make rolled candles

1 Drop a wick length into the wax, stir it around for a few seconds and lift it clear with the pliers.

2 Take a dipped wick, arrange it along one edge of a wax sheet, so that one end protrudes by about 1 cm (½ in), and use your fingertips to roll the sheet into a tight cylinder.

3 Use a warm knife to weld the edge of the wax into place.

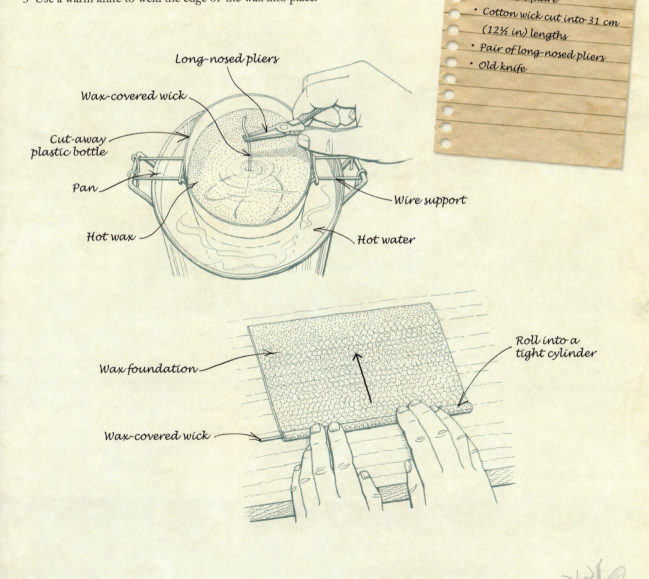

Long-nosed pliers

Wax-covered wick

Cut-away plastic bottle

Pan

Hot wax

Wire support

Hot water

Wax foundation

Wax-covered wick

Roll into a tight cylinder

Making soap and natural cleaning

Although more and more home-crafted soaps are being made from vegetarian ingredients such as cocoa fat and olive oil, there is now a lot of interest in the tradition of making soap from tallow (animal fat). It sounds a bit disgusting, but if you are a meat-eater or you are happy to use animal-based products then maybe it is good to face the fact that lots of kitchen and bathroom items were/are in some part made from tallow.

Making basic laundry soap from tallow

1 Put the minced fat and suet into a saucepan with water to cover and 5 tablespoons of salt, bring to the boil and simmer until you are left with a mix of liquid fat and crispy scraps of meat and gristle. Run the rendered fat through a sieve and save the waste for the garden birds. Repeat this procedure until you have enough tallow for the recipe.

2 Put the tallow into a clean pan and gently heat and melt.

3 Measure the water into a jug.

4 Measure the lye into another.

5 Pour the lye into the water and stir until clear. *Note: the lye must be poured into water – not the other way round.*

6 Pour this lye-water mixture into the melted tallow and stir until you reach trace – meaning when the mix comes together to the point of no return.

7 Pour into moulds, cover with clingfilm and leave overnight.

8 Remove the film and air-cure for 6–8 weeks.

MAKING LAUNDRY SOAP FROM TALLOW

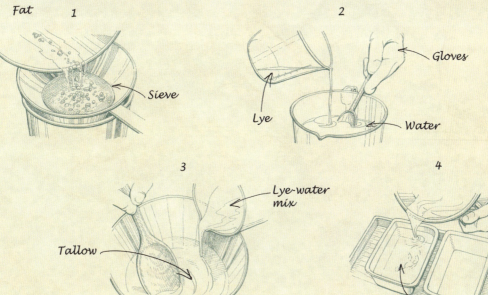

Fat

1

Sieve

2

Gloves

Lye

Water

3

Tallow

Lye-water mix

4

Pour into moulds

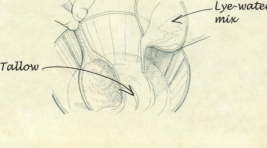

NATURAL CLEANING

- White vinegar - good as a disinfectant, will remove most bacteria and 80% of viruses.
- Lemon juice - good as a general-purpose cleaner of food-preparation surfaces.
- Tea tree oil - disinfects, kills mould, good as an antiseptic.
- Newspaper - scrunched-up newspaper is good for cleaning windows.

PETS, ANIMALS AND PARASITES

Certainly, pets and farm animals are carriers of disease and parasites, but contact with animals is in some way spiritually uplifting. Always keep the animals clean, keep pets away from the kitchen, and wash your hands after close contact with farm animals. If you have specific worries about animals and children, seek the advice of a vet.

Making teas and tisanes

A tea or tisane is a herbal drink designed to refresh, relax, stimulate or ease. To make it, boiling hot water is poured over the fresh or dried flowers, seeds, leaves or roots, and allowed to brew. Then the tea or tisane is strained, perhaps mixed with other ingredients such as honey or lemon juice, and served.

WARNING Just about everything that we ingest can cause allergic reactions. For example, I have an allergy to mushrooms, and coffee disagrees with Gill. Avoid anything that causes you problems.

Boiling water 1

Herbal infusion

Clean towel and strainer

Honey 2

Infused tea

Lemon

COMMON TEAS AND TISANES AND THEIR USES

- Artichoke - good for digestion and thought to lower cholesterol
- Barley tea - refreshing and used as a coffee substitute
- Barley water - wonderful summer drink, used to refresh and as a remedy for cystitis
- Catnip - used as a relaxant and sedative
- Chamomile - used as a laxative and sleep aid
- Chrysanthemum - used to lower fever, ease a sore throat and increase alertness
- Fennel - used to relax the intestines and ease wind and heartburn, thought to help lose weight
- Ginseng - used as a nourishing and pleasant stimulant and as a sexual 'pick-me-up'
- Mint - used to ease a sore throat, clear the tubes and as a mind-clearing drink
- Pine - refreshing and stimulating, the young green pine needles are served as tea
- Raspberries - used as a general tonic and relaxant, served to women in late pregnancy to ease labour
- Rosemary - used as a general 'pick-me-up'
- St John's Wort - traditionally used as a tonic for people suffering from mild depression
- Yarrow - used to ease arthritis, improve circulation and clear runny eyes

Making blackberry vinegar

My gran used to turn soft fruits like raspberries, blackcurrants and black-berries into fruit vinegars that she later served up as refreshing drinks or cough cures. The end product is not vinegary, but delicious and sweetly tart, like old wine. Kids love it.

Making blackberry vinegar

1   Gather the blackberries on a bright, sunny day when they are ripe, plump and at their best.

2   Remove the stalks, put the berries in a plastic or earthenware bowl, cover with good-quality malt vinegar and leave to stand for three days.

3   Strain through cotton muslin and leave to drip overnight.

4   Measure the juice into units of 500 ml (1 pint) and allow 450 g (1 lb) of organic sugar per unit.

5   Put the total juice-sugar mix into a stainless-steel pan and gently boil and simmer for no more than 5 minutes.

6   Skim off the scum, wait until the mix is cold, pour into wine bottles and cork securely. If you make it in late summer or autumn, it will be ready in winter.

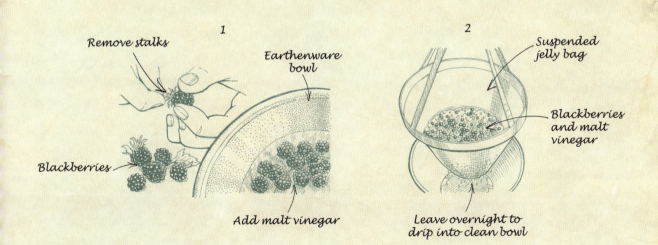

1

Remove stalks

Earthenware bowl

Blackberries

Add malt vinegar

2

Suspended jelly bag

Blackberries and malt vinegar

Leave overnight to drip into clean bowl

Building a kids' eco camp

An eco camp is a self-sufficient, off-grid place where your children can do their own thing. It might be an old shack in the woods, a shed, a small caravan, a tree house or whatever you like – as long as the kids see it as their own private space.

With self-sufficiency being at one with eco recycling, it follows that using salvaged structures and materials is good. We took a derelict shed and brought it to order with old windows, odds and ends of paint and all sorts of throwouts. As for the off-grid part, it depends upon where you live and how much time and effort you want to put in. We have built a rain collector, a wind turbine and a solar panel for lights. The kids still come back to the house for the toilet.

The costs depend upon your skills and the condition of the basic shed. If you look in your local newspaper, you will see that there are lots of old sheds out there. Our shed was in such a mess that the owners paid us to take it away.

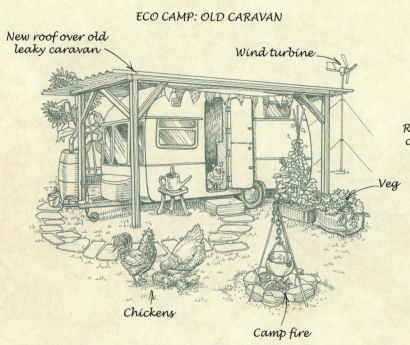

ECO CAMP: OLD CARAVAN

New roof over old leaky caravan

Wind turbine

Veg

Chickens

Camp fire

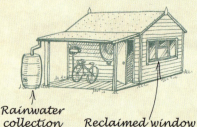

SHED VERSION 1

Rainwater collection

Reclaimed window

SHED VERSION 2

Canvas shade   Porch extension

INEXPENSIVE PORTABLE WORKBENCH

Vice jaws for clamping materials

Folding frame

Kids and tools

If we go with the legal definitions that define a child as any human being below the age of 18 and a hand tool as any device used for performing manual work on materials (wood, steel, paper, etc), then it is almost impossible to draw up meaningful guidelines.

As teachers and parents, Gill and I have always stated that children should only use tools under the guidance of a loving, caring and responsible adult. To put it another way, if you want your child to use a tool like a hammer or handsaw, you must always be present to guide them.

It is pretty obvious to see that some tools are more dangerous than others. For example, while we would selectively allow children under our care to use compasses, darning needles, scissors, spades, trowels, handsaws, knives, paintbrushes, sewing machines, spanners, wheelbarrows and the like – many of which are potentially dangerous – we would NEVER allow them to use mains-powered tools or fuel-driven machines or tools.

What about children aged, say, 14–18? Our thinking, and that of most educationalists, is that if you introduce tools to your kids at the earliest possible age, then they will have time to develop good, responsible tool-handling skills. However, you must always follow the manufacturer's safety instructions.

HOMEMADE SAWHORSE

Ripping notch to assist sawing down the length (ripping) of a plank

22 in (56 cm)-high

SMALL WORKBENCH FOR GARAGE OR SHED

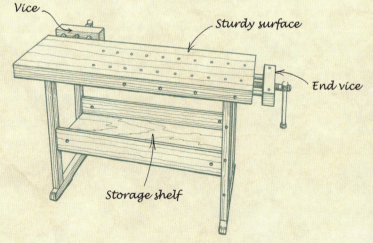

Vice

Sturdy surface

End vice

Storage shelf

Kids' food garden

A good swift way of getting children involved with self-sufficiency gardening is to encourage them to grow a few basic crops. We have chosen runner beans, potatoes and tomatoes because those are what we all like to eat, but you can grow whatever you like.

Jumbo bag and wigwam setup for runner beans

See page 82 for more information on growing runner beans.

1 Use the plastic tube to make a hoop that fits in the neck of the bag, and join the ends with the length of wood.

2 Sit the jumbo bag on the pallet and half-fill it with compost.

3 Put the hoop over the outside of the bag, fold the top down, and add more compost until the hoop is held in place.

4 Plant the bean seedlings about 23 cm (9 in) apart.

5 When the plants send out climbing tendrils, use the sticks to make a wigwam.

Jumbo bag for growing potatoes

See page 88 for more information on growing potatoes.

1 Cut the plastic tube to make a hoop to fit the neck of the bag, and join the ends with the length of wood.

2 Sit the jumbo bag on the pallet and half-fill it with compost.

3 Put the hoop over the outside of the bag, fold the top down so that the hoop is covered and add more compost until the bag starts to bulge.

4 Bang the iron fence rods in the ground, one at each corner of the bag.

5 Run the rope through the bag's loops, stretch the loops up to the irons and tie them off.

6 Use the needle and string to sew over-and-over the bag to the hoop.

7 Plant the potatoes about 23 cm (9 in) apart and 15 cm (6 in) deep.

Tomatoes

Home-grown tomatoes might be small and misshapen, but they taste wonderful – a bit like sweet cherries, only better. See page 94 for more information.

1   Fill the seed-tray with the potting compost and firm it level with your hands.

2   Sprinkle the seeds over the seed bed, cover them with a thin layer of compost, water with a fine spray, and cover with a sheet of glass topped with a newspaper.

3   When the seedlings are big enough to handle, take them one at a time and plant them in the 12 compost-filled pots.

4   Water the plants, give them a small liquid feed and transfer them to a warm, sheltered spot.

5   When the plants look too big for the pots, carefully remove them and plant them into the hanging basket or container.

6   Keep watering and feeding until the tomatoes look ready to be picked.

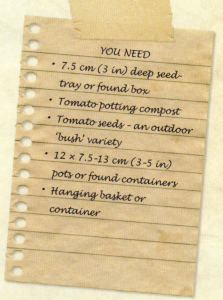

YOU NEED
- 7.5 cm (3 in) deep seed-tray or found box
- Tomato potting compost
- Tomato seeds – an outdoor 'bush' variety
- 12 × 7.5-13 cm (3-5 in) pots or found containers
- Hanging basket or container

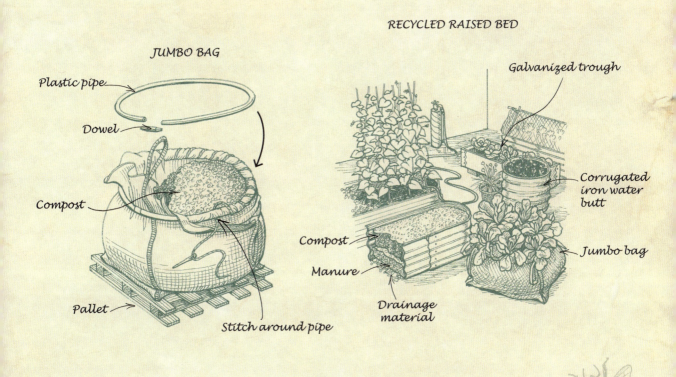

JUMBO BAG

Plastic pipe

Dowel

Compost

Pallet

Stitch around pipe

RECYCLED RAISED BED

Galvanized trough

Corrugated iron water butt

Jumbo bag

Compost

Manure

Drainage material

Toys

Toys As soon as our kids were old enough to hold, manage and understand tools (things like scissors, pencils, pliers and handsaws), we used to go out of our way to link their playtime pleasures into our self-sufficiency activities. If we built a shed, they built a den. If we put up a fence, they used leftover bits of wire to make some sort of toy. If we were doing woodwork, they had the offcuts, and so on.

Over the years they made everything from kites, treasure chests and tents to shelters, stilts, bows and arrows. Of course, partly we wanted to encourage and nurture their hands-on skills, but mostly we found that the best way of keeping them happy and out of mischief was to get them involved.

This go-kart is a good all-round starter project in that it can lead to all manner of useful trolleys, trucks, push carts and wheelbarrows.

Building a go-kart

1   Our design is made up of a wide, thick plank, a child's car seat, four battens, two threaded metal rods, a pair of bicycle wheels, a pair of trolley wheels and a few found bits and pieces.

2   Get your child to sit with legs bent and braced, just as if he/she were sitting on a kart, and measure the distance from the back of the seat to the feet.

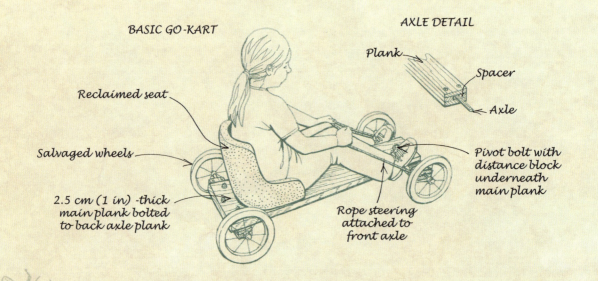

BASIC GO-KART

Reclaimed seat

Salvaged wheels

2.5 cm (1 in) -thick main plank bolted to back axle plank

Rope steering attached to front axle

AXLE DETAIL

Plank

Spacer

Axle

Pivot bolt with distance block underneath main plank

3 Saw the main plank to length accordingly.

4 Back wheels – sandwich the metal axles between the battens and screw the whole thing to the main plank.

5 Front wheels – fix the front axle to the front battens as described above.

6 Set the front wheel unit in place on the main plank and drill a pivot hole through the various layers.

7 Pass the bolt through the pivot hole, with washers sandwiched between wood, and use two or more nuts to clench up.

8 Screw your chosen seat to the back end of the main plank.

9 Fit the wheels on the axles.

10 Knot the steering rope in place.

Bicycles and children

When our kids were young and we were living in deep-mud country, bicycles were vital. If they wanted to visit friends, if we all wanted to go off on a picnic trip, or if I needed to transport some broken car bit to the garage, we used bicycles. A bicycle can be pushed through mud and water, lifted over a fence, wheeled along a track, lifted onto a truck, put on a train and easily mended. A bicycle can be pedalled along at speeds of 13–32 kph (8–20 mph), so you can easily cycle three times further than you can walk. If you live in the country, you need a bicycle. However, if you really want to realize your bicycle's full potential and use it to move bulky packages and weights, it needs to be fitted with a trailer.

NOTE Our trailer draws its inspiration from a bamboo-type trailer, as designed by the world-famous bike trailer company Carry Freedom. Our description and drawings cover the basics but, if you want to stay with the Carry Freedom designs, see their website (www.carryfreedom.com).

BIKE AND CARRY FREEDOM BAMBOO TRAILER

Trailer base created from numerous lengths of bamboo fixed to the frame

How to build and fit a trailer

1 Collect together all your materials and lay them out on the ground.

2 Cut, drill and bolt together the eight bamboo lengths that make the basic frame.

3 Make and fit the metal brackets that make the wheel carriers.

4 Fit the hitch as shown.

5 Look at the drawing and see how the frame is held square by tension wires that fit across the diagonals. These can be tension twisted, or fitted with turnbuckle adjusters.

6 Fit a box, net or rack to suit your carrying needs.

7 Fit the wheels, and fix the trailer to your bike's back wheel spindle.

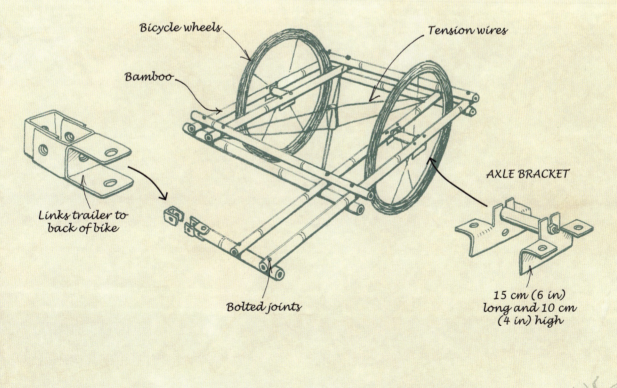

TRAILER

Bicycle wheels

Tension wires

Bamboo

Links trailer to back of bike

Bolted joints

AXLE BRACKET

15 cm (6 in) long and 10 cm (4 in) high

Bicycle wind turbine

This project draws its inspiration from a pre-war book that describes how to build wind turbines from old bicycles. The idea is beautifully direct: you take an existing dynamo hub wheel and replace the rim and spokes with blades. The wind blows the blades and the spinning dynamo generator powers up the lights.

Considering the design

The project is made from five component parts: the wheel hub dynamo, the blades and boss, the mounting block and tail, the tower, and the light.

Thinking about education

There is a lot of interest in wind energy. Your kids could use this project as a starting point for one of their science or engineering assignments.

How to build the wind turbine

1 Study your garden and fix the position of the wind turbine so that it is well away from overhanging wires and cables.

2 Take one length of pipe at a time and saw it lengthways, so that you finish up with four identical half-pipe pieces.

3 Measure the diameter of your dynamo hub and use compasses and saw to make two discs of plywood to fit. Sandwich the flange edge of the dynamo between the plywood discs and fix with a ring of screws.

4 Set the compasses to the radius of the plywood and step off six equidistant points around the diameter. Use alternate points to fix the position of the three blades.

BLADE DETAIL

Plastic pipe is cut in half …

… and trimmed to shape

5   Drill holes through the blades and plywood discs, and bolt the blades in position.

6   Bolt a U-shaped metal bracket to the hub spindle. Drill holes through the ends of the U-bracket that are slightly larger than the diameter of your mast.

7   Fix the tail vane in place with wire, jubilee clips and amalgamating tape.

8   Run two electric cables down from the dynamo hub contacts.

9   Fit the turbine on top of the mast, set the mast in place on the ground and secure the whole thing with guy ropes.

10 Wire the electric cables up to your chosen light. Wait for the wind to blow.

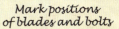

PLYWOOD DISC X 2

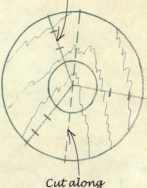

Mark positions of blades and bolts

Cut along this line

FRONT VIEW

Hub dynamo sandwiched between the plywood discs

Bolts

Plywood disc

Mast

SIDE VIEW

Plywood discs

Hub dynamo

Tail

An alternative way of mounting the turbine using a T-joint

Electric cable inside the mast

Jubilee clip

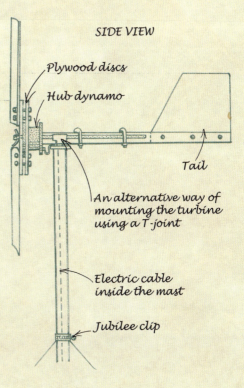

Camp-fire cooking

Camp-fire cooking A lot of self-sufficiency involves gardening, managing stock, building structures, cutting wood and such like, so there are lots of occasions when the swiftest, easiest and most pleasurable option is to light a fire and cook and eat out of doors. If you take this logic one step further and recognize that most adventurous kids will, sooner or later, have an urge to cook on a real pioneer-type fire, it is a good idea to proactively show them how to build just the right camp fire and how to cook a few basic meals.

What is a camp-fire circle?

It is an area where you can light a fire in relative safety. If you look at the illustrations, you will see that the circle is made up of a central fire pit, an inner ring of rocks or bricks, and an outer raised ring of turf. The users can sit on the outer raised area with their feet braced against the stones, in such a way that they can cook without coming to harm.

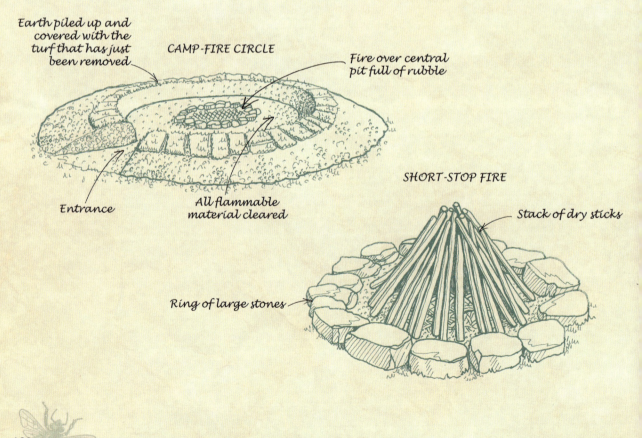

Earth piled up and covered with the turf that has just been removed

CAMP-FIRE CIRCLE

Fire over central pit full of rubble

Entrance

All flammable material cleared

SHORT-STOP FIRE

Stack of dry sticks

Ring of large stones

Short-stop fire

This is the sort of fire you need when you are so short of time that you only want to swiftly heat up some water for a pot of tea or soup and/or fry an egg. It is such an easy fire to build that you can be drinking and eating hot food in the space of half an hour. Build a tight ring of bricks or rocks in the centre of the fire circle, fill it with scrunched-up newspaper topped off with a cone of dry twigs, and start the fire. Once the fire is under way, simply bed the kettle or pan in the centre of the embers and start cooking.

Overnight cooking fire

This is the sort of fire you make when you and the kids want to spend a day and night camping and cooking around a good, solid, safe fire. Set two flat-topped green logs side by side in the centre of the fire circle, about 30 cm (12 in) apart. Then use an axe and a knife to make the crutch-pole-and-hanger arrangement so that is aligned with the logs, and light the fire as already described. The good thing about this fire is that there is enough room for you to boil a kettle, set up a frying pan and have a stew simmering.

Overnight comfort fire

This is the sort of fire you make when you are bone weary and want to do no more than doze in front of a warming fire, maybe boil a kettle and make a bit of toast. Build the little bed-and-back arrangement in the centre of the fire circle, cover it with turf and earth and then light the fire. The idea is that the earth gets so red hot that it throws the heat towards you and the open tents.

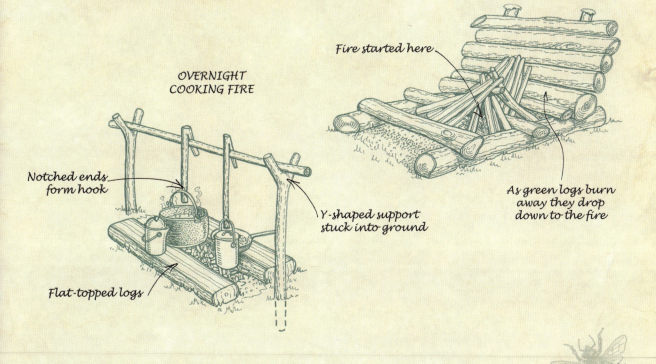

OVERNIGHT
COMFORT FIRE

Fire started here

OVERNIGHT
COOKING FIRE

Notched ends
form hook

Y-shaped support
stuck into ground

As green logs burn
away they drop
down to the fire

Flat-topped logs

Foraging

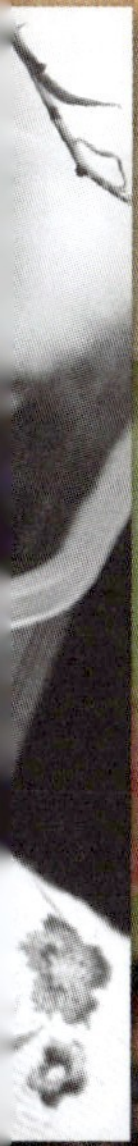

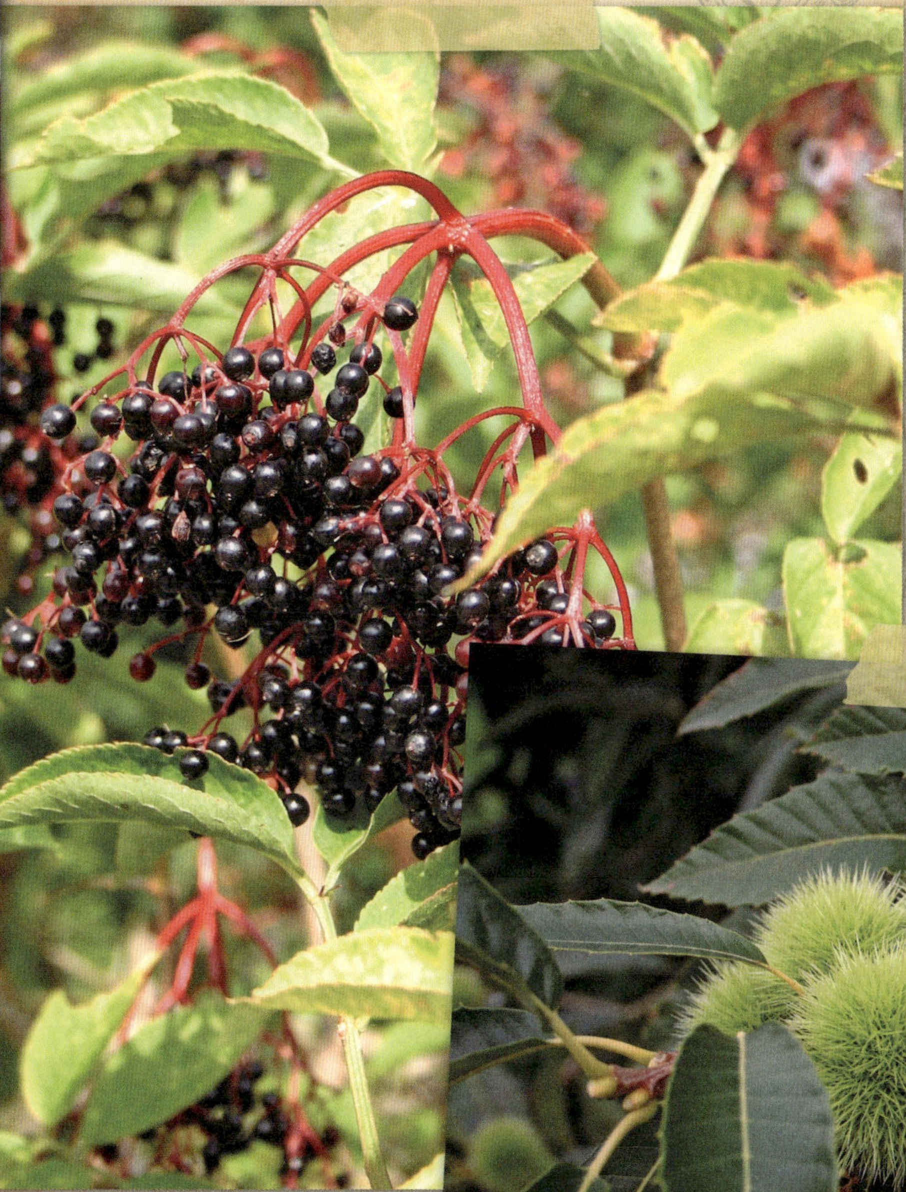

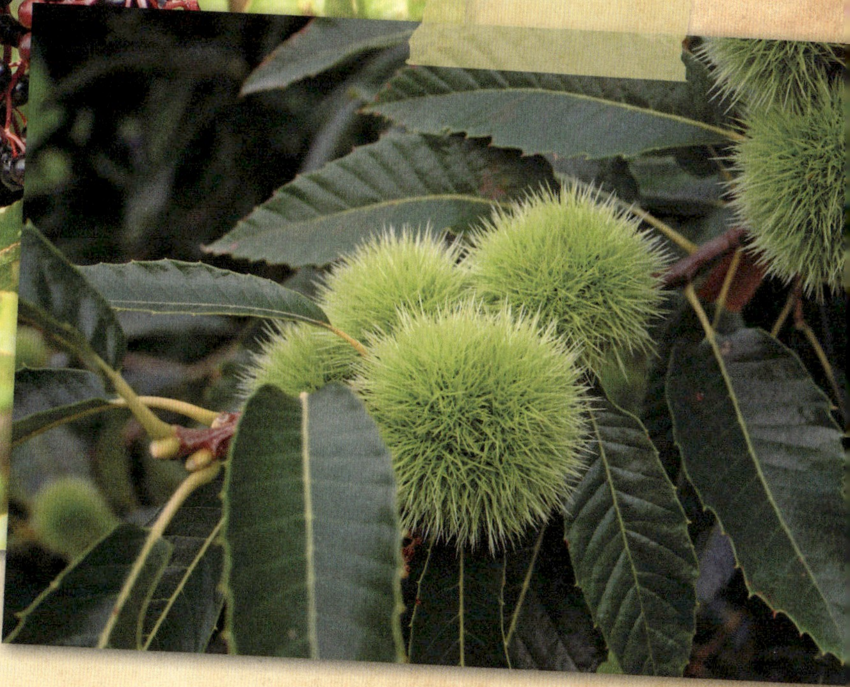

Foraging for wild berries

When I was a kid in the late 1950s, when citrus fruits like limes, lemons and oranges were difficult to obtain, the government set up poster campaigns to encourage churches and schools to collect wild fruits such as blackberries and rosehips. As I remember, the posters said that 30 rosehips contained as much vitamin C as 40 oranges.

Foraging and self-sufficiency

Although collecting wild fruits has always been part of traditional seasonal activities, the tricky and sometimes humorous business of dealing with the thorns has long been recognized – so much so that in Shakespeare's time brambles and blackberries were called 'lawyers' and vice versa, because when poor old Mr Everyman became entangled in their thorny embrace they would not let go until they drew blood.

If you aim to be self-sufficient, foraging for wild fruits and berries should figure highly. After all, it does not make any sense to buy in very expensive commercially grown blackberries or raspberries, for example, when there is an abundance of delicious, healthy, wild, organic fruits and berries in just about every wild thicket free for the picking.

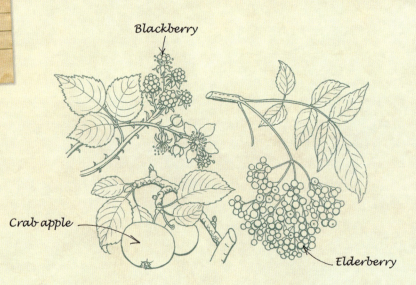

Blackberry

Crab apple

Elderberry

Edible berries

RASPBERRY There are all manner of red and black wild raspberries; the fruit looks a bit like a non-shiny version of a blackberry, good for jellies and jams.

BLACKBERRY Blackberries and brambles are amazingly good for jellies and jams, especially when mixed with apples.

DEWBERRY Looks a bit like a small, tight blackberry, and can be used in much the same way.

STRAWBERRY Very small strawberry, not much bigger than a redcurrant, grows on sunny banks; we always eat them freshly picked.

ROSEHIP The fruit of the wild rose, a long, rosy-red barrel shape; we mince and boil them in water, sieve them and mix the resulting liquid with sugar to make a tasty syrup that is a wonderful treatment for colds and sore throats.

SLOE A dark black-blue berry, the fruit of the blackthorn; we spike them and mix with sugar, put the whole lot into bottles and top up with gin to make an amazingly tasty alcoholic drink that we have always called 'pink gin'.

ROWAN The berry of the Rowan or Mountain Ash, a smooth, red-orange berry that grows in hanging clusters; can be turned into a syrup or jelly in much the same way as rosehips.

CRAB APPLE Looks like a small green-orange apple, tastes sharp; we generally boil them up in water and turn them into a thick jelly that we use to sweeten ground rice milk puddings.

REDCURRANT Looks like a miniature pip-filled garden redcurrant; there are so many pips in fact that it is best boiled with water, sieved, mixed with sugar and turned into a jelly.

GOOSEBERRY Looks like a green-yellow-orange gooseberry; we think they are best mixed with apples and turned into jam.

ELDERBERRY A blue-black-purple colour, grows in hanging clusters; it can be made into a jelly, and we also use the flowers to make what we call 'elderflower champagne' – a very fizzy, nicely heady and refreshing drink.

DANDELION

CHICKWEED

NETTLE

Foraging for wild greens

In the context of this book, 'greens' are just about anything from salad leaves and stinging nettles through to seaweed and salad herbs that can variously be eaten raw or cooked.

The way it was

When I was a kid, eating foraged greens was so commonplace that when my gran told me to get a bit of salad for lunch I simply wandered down the huge wild garden, picked a few leaves of watercress, a handful of dandelion leaves or whatever I found, gave them a swift rinse under the tap and put them on the table alongside bread, chutney and cheese. The following list is no more than a taster – there are hundreds to choose from.

WATERCRESS Looks like shop-bought cress, found in slow-running fresh water streams; wash it well.

LIME Young leaves of the linden tree; wash and eat with bread and cheese.

HAWTHORN Sometimes called 'Bread and cheese'; the young shoots and leaves are best eaten in salad with brown bread and olive oil.

DANDELION The young leaves can be eaten with bread and butter, very tasty.

CHICKWEED Best picked as a handful and cooked with chopped onions and olive oil; can also be eaten as a relish with bread and cheese, or alongside meat or fish.

STINGING NETTLE Best finely chopped or minced and cooked along with onions and garlic to make a beautiful soup.

KELP Looks like flat, slimy ribbons; can be eaten with salad leaves or used finely chopped to thicken a soup.

WILD CELERY Pungent plant that looks very much like shop-bought celery; best washed and dried and added to soups.

Foraging for wild nuts

While foraging is fun in itself, looking for nuts is especially exciting in that they have a high food value. So, while salad leaves can be used to enrich a main meal, a helping of nuts can in itself be a main meal.

SWEET CHESTNUTS Of all the nuts, these are the one that just about everyone knows – the shiny brown nuts are enclosed in a very spiky, green, difficult-to-handle outer case. We generally steam our chestnuts and turn them into a delicious nut roast.

HAZELNUTS The long and shiny nuts are contained in a cap-like outer case. Every year there is a competition between us and the squirrels, and we usually lose. I prefer to eat them raw.

BEECHNUTS Four little quarter nuts fit together inside an outer husk. We either eat ours raw or steam and mash them to add to a nut roast.

WALNUTS On the tree, the nuts look green and conker-like. We wait until they are ready and eat them raw.

ACORNS Although in times past acorns were roast, crushed, washed and variously eaten as a coarse-ground meal and as a substitute for coffee, in the context of self-sufficiency they are best left on the ground as food for turkeys or pigs.

HAZELNUTS

BEECHNUTS

SWEET CHESTNUTS

COCKLE

Foraging for wild seashore food

If you live near the sea and enjoy beachcombing, you will love foraging for seashore food. Be aware that there are restrictions in some countries on precisely what you can forage from the seashore. That said, common law rights in most countries permit the right to forage for shellfish in tidal waters.

COCKLES They look like a hinged pair of fan-shaped shells, and can be hand-gathered all year round. Soak in salt water overnight, boil in water and eat with salt and vinegar.

MUSSELS These look like a pair of hinged, blue-black shells, and can be hand-gathered in autumn. Simmer in a covered pan with olive oil and garlic, and eat with brown bread and butter.

RAZOR CLAMS Although there are all manner of clams, it is the long razor clam that is best recognized. It looks like of a pair of long, hinged blades, a bit like an old-fashioned cut-throat razor. They can be dug out of the sand from late spring through to late summer. Boil in water, simmer the fleshy foot in olive oil and add to a fish stew.

WINKLE

WINKLES They look like the archetypal snail with a blue-black shell, and can be gathered from pools and rocks in all but the summer months. Boil in water for 10 minutes, get the flesh out with a pin and eat sprinkled with salt and vinegar.

SLIPPER LIMPET

SLIPPER LIMPETS These are most often seen thrown up on the beach as a little stack of shells stuck one to another, and can be gathered from late spring to late summer. Boil in water for about 15 minutes, then add the fleshy lump to a fish stew to give a chewy interest.

MUSSEL

RAZOR CLAM

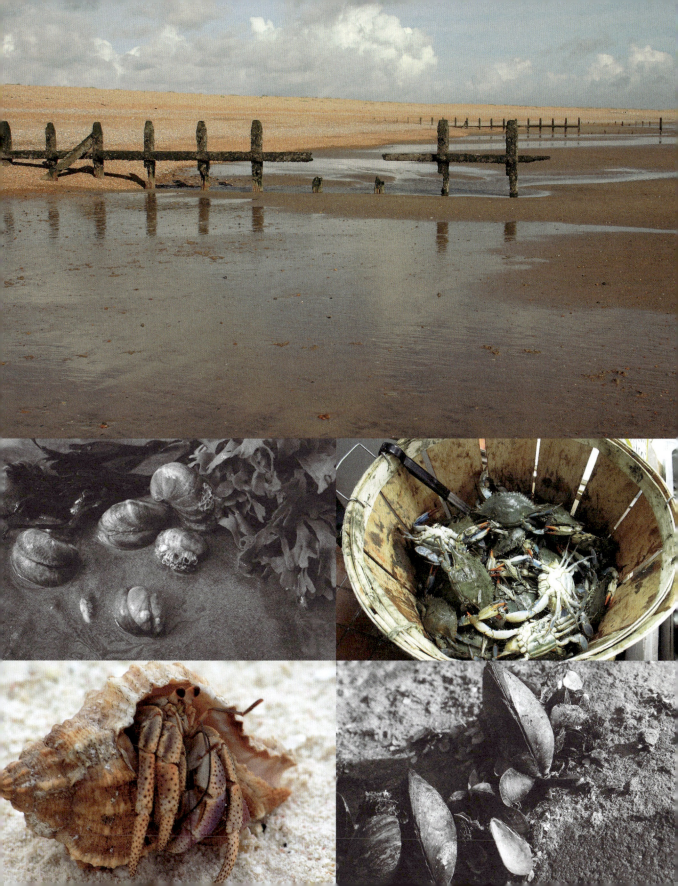

Snaring live rabbits in a bushcraft spring net

When we first started out in self-sufficiency, every other farmer and country worker caught rabbits for the pot. They simply set home-made slip-loop-type snares in holes in hedges and fences and ate their catch.

Bushcraft spring nets

A bushcraft spring net trap is made with a knife and an axe out in the field from a sprung sapling or branch, a length of twine and a loose net. The rabbit walks onto the net and pulls at the bait, with the effect that the little trip-hook mechanism slips from its catchment to release the sprung sapling, which in turn raises and closes the net. The object of the exercise is to catch the rabbit alive so that you can humanely dispatch it for the pot.

WARNING If you set such a trap, you must check it at regular intervals.

RABBIT SNARE

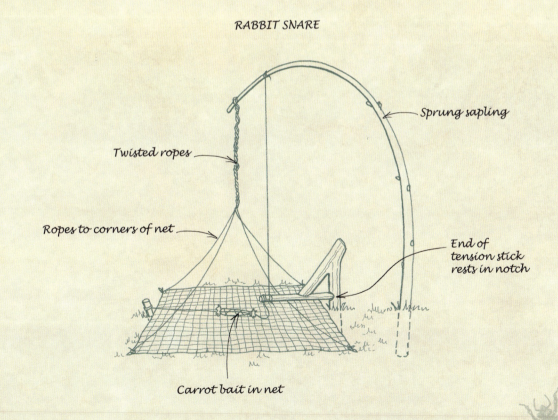

Sprung sapling

Twisted ropes

Ropes to corners of net

End of tension stick rests in notch

Carrot bait in net

Shooting rabbits for the pot

Our plot is overrun with hundreds of wild rabbits. We shoot them for their meat and so our geese have more grass.

Using a gun

• Never shoot if you are anxious, tired or medicated.

• Only shoot when the rest of the family are safely out of the way.

• Make sure that if you overshoot your target the shot or pellet is going to hit seen ground.

• Never shoot into woodland or towards a public right of way.

• Take your time, hold the gun firmly into your shoulder, slip the safety catch, sight the target and squeeze the trigger.

AIR RIFLE A top-quality .22 air rifle is a good, relatively low-cost option. You do not need a licence, you can kill at a good distance and it does not make much noise.

SHOTGUN I use a shotgun from spring to late winter, when the ground is firm, green and silent underfoot. When I cannot get within shotgun range because the ground is carpeted with crunchy leaves, I use the air rifle.

Skinning and preparing a rabbit

1 Use a sharp knife to cut off the feet, head and tail.

2 Hold the rabbit up by a pinch of back fur and use the knife to remove a track of fur from head to tail.

3 Use two hands to pull the fur off from the back around to the belly.

4 Hold the rabbit up by its back, with the tail end hanging over a bowl. Being careful not to pierce the guts, cut in from the belly down towards the tail so that gravity drops the rabbit's guts into the bowl.

5 Save the lungs, heart and kidneys and wash the rabbit.

Woodcraft

Fences, hurdles and gates

When we first came here, there was a broken-down fence all around on the outside of the hedge and a single farm gate into the main field, and that was about it. Over the last three years, we have built a rabbit-proof fence around the vegetable garden, an easy-to-move electric mesh fence around the geese field, a low wire fence around the apiary, and a new stock wire fence around the whole plot, and we also have a lot of loose gates and hurdles that we use to create temporary enclosures. If you intend to keep stock, you will need good fences and gates. If you share a fence or gate with a neighbour, you should communicate before you even think about making changes.

FENCES A fence can be functional, attractive, made of posts and wire mesh, made of wooden posts and rails, and so on. You need to establish what you want the fence to do and build the fence accordingly.

HURDLES A hurdle is a movable metal or wooden barrier that can be used to create temporary enclosures.

GATES Gates come in all shapes, sizes, styles and materials. Permanent main gates must have good, easy-to-swing hinges and positive latches.

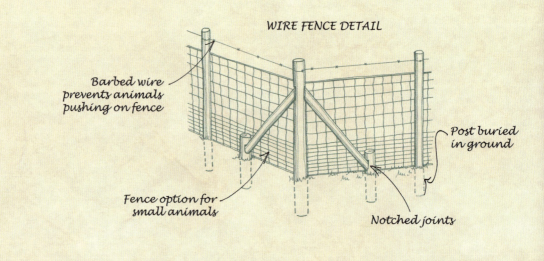

WIRE FENCE DETAIL

Barbed wire prevents animals pushing on fence

Post buried in ground

Fence option for small animals

Notched joints

Outbuildings

Outbuildings If you have ambitions to be self-sufficient, you will almost certainly have to build a number of sheds, shelters, lean-tos and shacks. To date, we have built a rough shed for storing the logs, a smart workshop for woodworking, an eco shed for the kids to sleep in, a shed with a lean-to on the side for the geese, a lean-to against the back door in which to leave boots and coats, and a shed for the vegetable garden. I am not even finished – I still have to build a pole-type barn shelter for the tractor. The challenge is that every shed and shelter has to be designed to suit a particular need.

POLE BARN A pole barn is essentially a double-pitched, single-pitched or flat roof supported on poles. An open-sided shelter of this character is good for storing tractors and machinery and for working outside but under cover.

LEAN-TO SHELTER The big advantage of a lean-to shelter is that the costs are kept down, simply because such a shelter shares a wall and structural support with an existing shed or shelter. For example, when we discovered that our geese would not use the enclosed shed we had built for them, we built a lean-to shelter on the side of the shed. They now use the lean-to for shelter while we use the initial shed for storing feed and equipment.

VEGETABLE GARDEN SHED Having been disappointed by one or two poor-quality, factory-made, off-the-peg sheds, we decided to splash out on a custom-made shed. It is beautiful and well worth the extra cost. We fitted it out with a work surface, shelves and lots of hooks for tools.

LOG SHED The idea of our log shed is that the freshly cut logs can be tipped out in front of the shed and then easily barrowed in and stored. The open structure at base and roof level allows for good airflow to dry out the wood, the large roof overhang keeps off the rain, and the wide doorway allows for easy wheelbarrow access.

POST FOUNDATIONS FOR A SHED

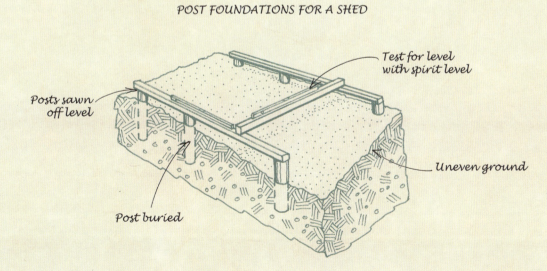

Test for level
with spirit level

Posts sawn
off level

Post buried

Uneven ground

Sawing and stacking wood

If you have a woodburning stove and access to a bit of woodland that needs thinning, tidying up and coppicing, you are probably going to need to use a chainsaw. You could use a handsaw and an axe, and we still do, but it is very hard work.

Our chainsaw

Although by choice we have one of the smallest modern petrol chainsaws on the market – the blade is only about 30 cm (1 ft) long – it is more than enough to cope with anything we need to cut.

Felling a small tree

1 Always aim to let a tree fall towards its natural angle of lean.

2 Cut a 30–45° notch on the side of the tree, on the side facing the direction of fall. The notch should run about one-third of the way into the diameter.

3 Move to the side of the tree furthest away from the notch, and make a final cut that runs about 2.5–5 cm (1–2 in) higher than the notch, so that there remains a good 'hinge' of wood about 3.5–5 cm (1½–2 in) thick between the final cut and the point of the notch.

4 Turn off the saw and put it out of harm's way.

5 Take your logging bar (sometimes called a breaking bar), push it into the third cut and apply pressure.

6 When you see the tree gradually start to lean in towards the notch, move backwards well away from the stump.

7 Use the chainsaw to remove all the branches from the tree.

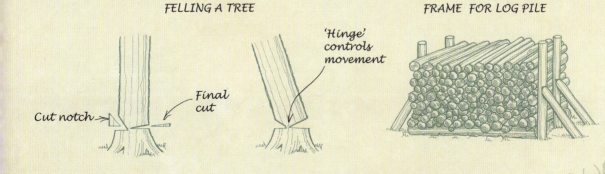

FELLING A TREE

Cut notch →

Final cut

'Hinge' controls movement

FRAME FOR LOG PILE

Chopping wood

A big misconception about using an axe to split logs and a hatchet to split kindling is that it requires huge strength. It does not. Gill and I are getting old and we manage it nicely. The trick is to have a good slice of tree for a chopping block, good, sharp, well-balanced tools, a keen eye and a nice heap of straight-grain wood, and to be coolly focused.

Method for splitting logs

1 Dress for the task – heavy shoes, thin leather gloves and goggles.

2 Position the chopping block so there is clear ground all around – no overhanging trees, buildings or greenhouses.

3 Set the sawn log on the chopping block so that the end grain is uppermost.

4 Take your medium-weight, long-handled, two-handed axe, set the blade edge on the log to be split, stand your distance with your feet comfortably apart, and check that both hands have a firm hold.

5 Look around to check that all the family – kids, partner, granny, dogs and cats – are out of harm's way and the ground is firm and free from debris.

6 Lift the axe with an easy swinging motion – no huge grunts or great effort – and bring the blade down on the log. If you have got it right, the log will split.

Method for chopping kindling with a hatchet

1 Position the chopping block at a comfortable working height. Put the wood to be worked on the chopping block. Hold the wood with one hand and set the blade of the hatchet on the wood.

2 Now, at the same time, lift both the wood and the hatchet slightly and bring them down so that wood hits the chopping block and the weight of the hatchet runs on through to split off kindling.

3 When you are practised, you will be able to work at a comfortable speed, with one hand supporting the wood to be split and the other slicing away with the hatchet.

SPLITTING LOGS

CHOPPING KINDLING

Charcoal

If your vision of self-sufficiency includes having a plot of land, cutting logs for a woodburning stove, lots of cooking and eating out of doors, perhaps having a tractor and generally putting ironwork to rights, then making charcoal will fit neatly into your scheme.

What is charcoal?

Charcoal is the characteristically soft, brittle, black-grey, lightweight stuff that is left when you burn wood in the absence of oxygen. To put it another way, if you set light to a heap of wood and then cover up the burning heap to restrict the oxygen and hold back the burning, the end product will be charcoal.

Making charcoal in an oil drum

1 Take the drum and use the hammer and cold chisel to cut out one end and to punch a dozen or so holes in the other end.

2 Set the drum, open end uppermost, on a ring of bricks.

3 Light a good fire in the drum and slowly top it up with log wood.

4 When the fire is well alight, put the sheet of steel on the top of the drum so that the top is three parts covered.

5 When, over the space of a couple of hours, the smoke turns from thick white to clear blue, completely cover the top of the drum and dig earth up against the base of the drum until all the air holes are well covered.

6 After 24 hours or so, when the drum and the contents are completely cold, up-end the drum to empty out the charcoal.

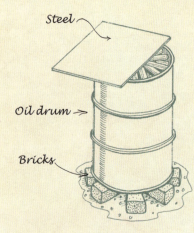

Steel

Oil drum

Bricks

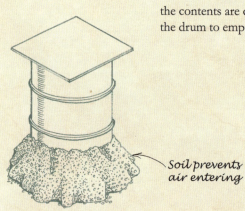

Soil prevents air entering

Whittling

The art of shaping wood with a knife might seem to be a bit 'Daniel Boone' and 'frontier woodsman', but the fact is that using a knife to slice and shape wood is an activity that will almost certainly feature in your self-sufficiency lifestyle.

What can you make?

Over the last year or so, I have whittled a bit of oak to make a folksy catch for a cupboard, made a toggle for a motor pump pull-rope, sharpened some pegs in the garden, made a whistle for the kid next door, made an apple stomper, and made a new handle for a kitchen knife.

Techniques

SLICING ACTION Hold the work piece in one hand while slicing away from your body with the knife held in the other hand.

PUSH-PARING ACTION Hold the work piece in one hand while 'thumb paring' away from your body with your elbow tucked into your waist to make a tight, controlled cut.

PULL-PARING ACTION Hold the work piece in one hand with the thumb of the other hand pushed against the work piece while making an 'apple paring' cut.

CAUTION
- A whittling knife is a potentially dangerous tool - used incorrectly it can cause severe injury
- First-timers should seek training from a competent professional before using a whittling knife
- Keep a first-aid kit near to hand

PUSH-PARING ACTION

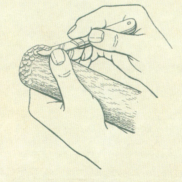

PULL-PARING ACTION

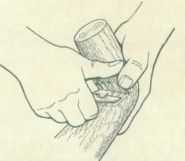

SLICING ACTION

Resources

www.direct.gov.uk/en/environmentandgreenerliving
UK government site with tips for recycling, energy saving, vegetable growing, keeping livestock and much more.

http://carboncalculator.direct.gov.uk
Calculate your carbon footprint.

www.decc.gov.uk
Department of Energy and Climate Change.

www.energysavingtrust.org.uk
UK organization helping save energy and reduce carbon emissions.

www.defra.gov.uk
UK government department distributing information and setting out policies involving the environment, food and rural affairs.

www.countrysmallholding.com
The Country Smallholding magazine site.

www.epa.gov
US Environmental Protection Agency.

www.epa.gov/climatechange/kids
A Student's Guide to Global Climate Change.

http://globe.gov
The Global Learning and Observations to Benefit the Environment (GLOBE) program is an education program for schools.

http://gcmd.nasa.gov
NASA's Global Change Master Directory (GCMD). Giving everybody access to information relevant to global change.

www.nrel.gov
National Renewable Energy Laboratory.

www.backwoodshome.com
The Backwoods Home Magazine site.

Index